Praise for
Awakening the Hero Within

After reading *Awakening the Hero Within* my first thought was WOW! What a gift to all men, married or single. Wives and families will benefit when dads read this book. Teko speaks to the struggles most fathers face with biblical truths, amazing sensitivity, incredible love, encouragement and insight. His transparency is inspiring. I'll read a chapter a week for quite some time. You can't just read this book once— it has too much spiritual gold to process in one reading.

—Dr. Clarence Shuler
President/CEO BLR: Building Lasting Relationships

Imagine who you want your kids to become. Be that. This is easier said than done. My friend Teko identifies many challenges that prevent us men from achieving this profound goal—the monotony of routine, the weight of expectations, the debilitation of fear and disappointment, and the times when, despite our best efforts, God is or seems silent. But this book is a call to resilience—to set aside striving and anxiety and trust in the immense love and inscrutable sovereignty of our Father for each one of us. Over time He does shape our identity, affirm our purpose and establish our legacy. I wholeheartedly recommend Awakening the Hero Within because it truly is not just a book . . . but an invitation!

—Dr. Ralph Edward Plumb
https://drralphplumb.com

Every man I know is carrying more than he lets on. This book names it—the loneliness, the pressure, the spiritual emptiness that builds when we try to lead alone. Teko cuts through the myth of the lone hero and reminds us that real strength is built in community. Suffering may shape us, but brotherhood sustains us. This isn't a theory, it's a practical, honest guide to showing up for the men in your life and letting them show up for you. I recommend this book wholeheartedly to pastors, mentors, and any man ready for lasting transformation.

—Pastor German Ricca, Harvest Church, Omaha
Mentorlink – GproCommission

Teko Bailey speaks directly to the quiet battles men carry— pressure, performance, inherited ceilings, and the ache for meaning. With wisdom and authenticity, he helps men realign their lives around faith, brotherhood, and purpose. *Awakening the Hero Within* is a timely and needed roadmap for any man who wants to lead well, live free, and leave a legacy that lasts.

—Dr. Chris Harper
Chief Storyteller & CEO Betterman

If you've ever felt stuck between who you are and the man you truly want to be, this book will meet you there. Teko shows us that strength isn't about having it all together— it's about staying anchored when everything feels uncertain. This is a must-read for any man ready to stop drifting and start living with purpose, courage, and grace.

—Mitch Matthews
Coach, Speaker & Podcaster

AWAKENING THE
HERO
WITHIN

AWAKENING THE

HERO WITHIN

A MAN'S GUIDE TO STRENGTH, FAITH, AND PURPOSE

TEKO BAILEY

Awakening the Hero Within

Copyright © 2026 by Teko Bailey

The views and opinions expressed in this book are those of the author and do not necessarily reflect the official policy or position of Illumify Media Global.

Published by

Illumify Media Global

www.IllumifyMedia.com

"Let's bring your book to life!"

Library of Congress Control Number: 2026904938

Paperback ISBN: 978-1-970582-05-5

Cover design by Debbie Lewis

Printed in the United States of America

To Kalino and Kawika
May you always walk in strength, purpose and grace.

Contents

Foreword

Have you ever asked yourself, "Do I have what it takes…? To lead my family? To lead a team of highly competent people? To lead myself?" If so, then this book is for you. Easy to read, it will give you courage to step up in any area where you desire to see personal growth, and guide you in discovering answers to some of the big questions in life.

Teko Bailey shares some profound and eternal truths, and gives some simple ways to apply them. They work and are doable. Over a lifetime of embracing divine principles, he has tested and proved them in his own life. Ask his wife. Ask his friends. The same God will work for you as He yearns to bring blessing in your life. No matter where you come from, or what challenges you may be facing, you will be a better person to those you seek to love and lead if you read and apply what he has written. This book is about multiplication. No one lives in a bubble; the ripple effect will extend to the lives of many in your circles of influence. The timeless concepts Teko explores will help bring to you the transformation you hunger for, and give you keys to becoming an agent of change in your world.

I'm a septuagenarian and I've proven these principles over the years! I've seen them at work in Teko's life too.

It might not be easy; it won't be quick, but application of the truths in this book will bring a maturity and confidence that you, I, and every human on our planet hungers to experience.

—Jim Orred
Leadership coach

A Note to the Reader

You picked up this book for a reason. Maybe it was curiosity, maybe it was recommendation, or maybe—just maybe—it's because something in you is ready for more.

This is not just a book. It's an invitation.

You won't find perfection here. You'll find stories, reflection, scripture, challenge, and grace. You'll find a brother walking beside you—not a teacher shouting from a distance.

This book was written with you in mind. Whether you're on the mountaintop or in the valley, wrestling with purpose or pressing forward in faith, I hope every page speaks directly to your heart and stirs your spirit.

Let's grow together. Let's rise together.

Introduction

Discovering the Hero Within

John Eldredge, in his book *Wild at Heart*, tells the story of a young boy perched high in a tree. With a mixture of courage and hesitation, the boy calls out to his father below, "Dad, are you watching?" Without missing a beat, his father replies, "I'm watching, son. Go for it."[1]

That boy's cry, "Are you watching?" is one we've all echoed, whether we've realized it or not. Deep within every man lies a desire to be seen, encouraged, and believed in—a longing for permission to go after the life we were created for. But how often do we, as men, silence that voice? We settle into routines, trade boldness for caution, and bury the hero within under the weight of expectations, disappointments, or fear.

What if you could hear your Heavenly Father's voice, calling to you today? What if He is watching, cheering you on, and saying, "Go for it"?

You may not feel like a hero right now. Maybe life's challenges have left you doubting your strength, questioning your purpose, or struggling to see how God can use your story. But I want to assure you: the hero is still there.

---

[1] John Eldridge, Wild at Heart *Eldredge, J. (2001). Wild at Heart: Discovering the Secret of a Man's Soul. Thomas Nelson.*

At the core of every man's journey is this truth: you were made in the image of God, and your life was designed with purpose. The world will try to derail you from this truth, encouraging you to hide behind masks of invulnerability or false strength. But this book is your invitation to embrace the fullness of who you are—a courageous, creative, skillful warrior who leads and serves others, rooted in God's purpose and design.

WHY THIS JOURNEY MATTERS

The journey of a man isn't about perfection; it's about progress. It's about choosing to show up each day, even when it's hard, and trusting that God is at work in the midst of the challenges. You might be wondering, "Why now? Why this book?" Because the world needs men like you—men who are willing to embrace their purpose, lead with courage, and build a better legacy for the next generation.

As you read these pages, I encourage you to reflect on this question: *What legacy are you building today?*

Your answer doesn't have to be perfect, but it starts here—with a willingness to rediscover your strength, trust God in every season, and live with intentionality. Together, we'll explore the challenges and opportunities that shape you into the man you were meant to be.

Your Heavenly Father is watching. He sees you. He believes in you. Now it's time to believe in yourself.

Let's begin.

With anticipation and excitement,

Teko L.H. Bailey

chapter one

Finding Your Compass: Rediscovering Your Purpose

Many men carry a quiet ache, an internal pull toward something more—more than getting by, more than earning a paycheck, more than being admired for doing it all right on the outside while feeling adrift on the inside. It's the ache for direction—the desire to know that your life is actually aimed toward something meaningful.

Think of purpose like a compass. Now, imagine standing on a vast, uncharted terrain. The horizon stretches endlessly but offers no clear direction. You hold your compass in your hand, but the needle spins wildly, unable to settle. That's what life may feel like when you lack purpose: you're in motion, but you're drifting—not sure if you're moving toward anything that truly matters. Your days are full, but your soul is empty.

This is not the only kind of lost though. For some men, the compass works fine, but it's been stuffed in a pocket and ignored. At some point, you've stopped trusting it, or you've chosen to run in a different direction.

And then there are others, who instead of relying on a compass, are dependent on a map handed to them by culture, family, or ambition. But you've never stopped to ask if these maps are leading anywhere worth going.

I've been all three of those men. I've had seasons where the compass spun out. Seasons where I buried it beneath ambition. And seasons where I didn't even realize I needed one, until everything familiar fell apart. So, if that's where you are right now, I get it. Whatever your situation, the result is the same: a sense of misalignment. Something feels off, even if everything on the outside looks right.

This chapter is about recognizing that misalignment and reclaiming the internal compass that was designed to guide you. Whether you've drifted, resisted, or never knew your direction in the first place, the truth remains: you were made for purpose.

WHEN YOUR COMPASS SPINS: THE DRIFTER

You might identify with the man in the desert. You're holding your compass but north keeps shifting. One day, you feel clear and driven, the next, you're unsure if you're even on the right path. Life becomes a blur of motion: emails, meetings, commutes, routines—but little movement toward what truly matters. You're doing everything right, yet something inside feels off. That's the tension of a spinning compass, always active, rarely aligned.

Marcus knew that feeling well. By most standards, he had a good life: a steady job, a faithful marriage, two kids, and a reputation for being reliable. He showed up where it mattered. But deep down, he knew he was running on autopilot. His faith felt distant. His marriage was cordial but shallow. His kids were growing fast, and though he provided well, he wasn't present—not in the moments that shaped them most. His days were full, but his heart was hollow.

Then, one evening his six-year-old son, Noah, climbed into his lap and asked, "Dad, do you still pray at night?" The question stopped him cold. It wasn't meant as a challenge; it was a mirror. In that moment, Marcus realized that his son had noticed what he'd been trying to ignore: his drift from God's presence. He hadn't lost his sense of purpose overnight; he had slowly drifted away from the One who gives it.

That's how it often happens. Before a man loses his fire, he loses his focus. And before he loses his focus, he's lost the intimacy that once fueled his conviction. The drift rarely begins in the calendar or the career—it begins in the heart.

When we stop prioritizing time with God, everything else begins to lose clarity. Work becomes heavier. Relationships feel dull. Our sense of purpose starts to wobble. But when we seek first His presence, everything else realigns. That's not cliché; it's the order of heaven. Get the main thing right, and other things start to find their place.

**When God isn't prioritized,
everything else loses clarity.**

That night, after everyone had gone to bed, Marcus sat alone on the couch. No phone. No noise. Just a Bible and the weight of conviction. He didn't know what to say, so he cried—not tears of shame, but of longing. He whispered the simplest prayer he could: "God, remind me who I am again."

There was no lightning bolt moment, but something shifted. He got honest. He repented for his spiritual passivity. He asked for grace to lead his home again. In the weeks that followed, he didn't overhaul his life, but he rebuilt his rhythm. He woke up earlier to sit in silence and read Scripture. He joined a small men's prayer group. He put his phone away during dinner. He started praying with his wife again. And most importantly, he started showing up, not just physically, but spiritually.

One morning, while reading a short devotional with Noah before school, his son looked up and smiled. "Dad, you seem happy again."

That's when Marcus realized: when you find true north again, you don't just find direction for yourself, you help lead others there too. You point your family toward it.

WHEN YOUR COMPASS IS IN YOUR POCKET: THE RUNNER

Some men might not look lost, because they're running fast, but not in the direction they should be heading. They know where God's calling them, but the path ahead feels too costly. If The Drifter is unsure which way to go, The Runner knows exactly where he's supposed to be—but avoids it.

Jonah was that man. God told him to go to Nineveh, but instead, he boarded a ship sailing in the opposite direction. He wasn't confused about his calling; he was resisting it. Fear, frustration, pride, they all whispered the same lie:

"There must be an easier way." Maybe you've been there too. You know the conviction stirring beneath the surface, but you keep pushing it down. You fill your calendar, busy your hands, and drown out the whisper that's asking for surrender. You tell yourself it's bad timing, that the kids are too young, or that you'll make the change once things settle down. But deep down, you know it, the compass hasn't moved. You're just choosing not to look at it.

Jonah's story reminds us that resistance doesn't just stall our purpose—it stirs storms. His choice to run didn't only affect him; it put everyone in his boat at risk. The men rowing beside him found themselves fighting a storm they didn't create.

That's how running works. When we resist what God's asking of us, the people around us feel the turbulence. Our families sense the distance. Our teams feel the tension. Our souls grow restless because we're carrying the weight of disobedience disguised as busyness. But here's the grace: even in Jonah's rebellion, God pursued him. He sent the storm not to punish him, but to wake him. He sent the fish not to end him, but to redirect him. God's mercy doesn't quit when you run—it runs after you.

**Resisting God creates turbulence
for those around us.**

The storm was a mirror, not to shame him, but to show him what fear had been hiding.

Jonah didn't need a new direction; he needed a renewed conviction to walk the one God had already revealed. Maybe your storm isn't made of waves and wind, but of inner unrest—sleepless nights, frustration that nothing seems to satisfy, a sense you keep buried because it frightens you that you're meant for something more.

Here's what Jonah teaches us: God doesn't want your perfection; He wants your surrender. When Jonah finally stopped running and cried out from the belly of the fish, God didn't shame him. He listened. And He gave him another chance.

If you can see yourself in Jonah, take courage. You're not too far gone. God specializes in rerouting runners. Start where Jonah did: Be honest. Get quiet. Stop fighting the compass; it's not there to control you—it's there to guide you home. And when you stop running from your purpose, you'll find peace again in His presence, the kind of peace no amount of striving can produce.

But what happens when a man isn't drifting or running, and he's following a map that was never meant for him? That's where we turn next.

WHEN YOU'RE FOLLOWING THE WRONG MAP: THE IMITATOR

Some men aren't drifting or running; they're following the wrong map. They're sincere, hardworking, and even disciplined. But somewhere along the way, they started building their lives around the blueprints handed down to them—what culture, family, or tradition said a "successful man" should be. He's the man who's doing everything "right" but quietly wondering, Is this really what I was made for?

He's more limited than he is lost. His map is old, familiar, and safe. It worked for someone once, but it was never designed for him. Jonah ran from purpose. The imitator redefines purpose into something safer. He chooses predictability over possibility. He mistakes someone else's story for his own.

Maybe you were told that being a man means providing and keeping the peace—but never showing weakness. Maybe you grew up in a home where success meant stability, not surrender, where the goal was to manage life perfectly rather than trust God completely. Or perhaps faith was modelled as routine, not a relationship. Those maps gave you structure, but not direction.

The truth is God's purpose for you is not a recycled version of another man's. His compass doesn't lead backward into imitation—it leads forward into transformation. God's purpose is like new technology: precise, responsive, alive. It recalibrates when you drift and guides you through unfamiliar terrain. But you can't experience it if you're still unfolding someone else's outdated map.

Here's the good news: God has already placed a divine blueprint within you. Every man carries it. The problem is that most of us were never taught how to read it. Having the plans is one thing—knowing how to interpret and build from them is another. Without that clarity, we improvise. We build from memory, copy others, or rely on cultural templates. But hope isn't a strategy. And when the storms hit, only a life built on faith, identity, and purpose will stand.

So, if you find yourself walking a path that looks successful but feels hollow, pause. Ask God to show you the blueprint He's placed within you. Let Him exchange imitation for revelation. Because the life He's leading you toward might not look like the map you were handed—but it's the one that will finally make you come alive.

ALIGNING WITH YOUR COMPASS

Some men drift. Others run. And some spend their lives imitating what worked for someone else, only to find themselves weary, uncertain, and disconnected. These men may look like they have it all together—their compass in hand, their stride purposeful, and their schedules full. But, as I have mentioned, you can have motion without meaning. You can build a reputation, income, and even influence while quietly wondering whether any of it truly matters. What all these men have in common is misalignment: misaligned in rhythm, in focus, in identity. And that misalignment often happens, not always out of rebellion, but out of confusion.

I remember a season in my early twenties when I was sure I was headed in the right direction. I had just graduated from university with a degree in music education and a minor in communication. I loved people, I loved creativity, and I imagined building a future in music production and stage management, helping artists bring meaningful work to life. It felt like I was headed in the right direction. But looking back, I realize that even a good plan can become misaligned when it isn't anchored in God's direction.

A portion of my education at that time had been supported by my aunt and her husband—two generous, successful business owners who believed in my potential. For a time, their support felt like a gift. But as I began sensing God leading me toward opportunities that didn't align with their vision for my future, the relationship became strained. I was young and passionate but lacked the maturity to navigate that tension wisely. Eventually, I made a hard decision: I stepped away from their guidance. At the time, it felt like defiance, but in truth, it was the beginning of a deeper surrender. I wasn't rejecting wisdom; I was learning to trust God's compass for myself.

That choice led to a very difficult transition. I wasn't running from God, but I was being stripped of everything that once defined my sense of stability. I didn't have mentors who truly understood me, and I didn't yet have the spiritual maturity to see that God was using this season to build something in me. What felt like loss was actually realignment. The compass I had been following wasn't broken; I simply didn't yet know how to read it.

In that wilderness, God began rebuilding me from the inside out. It wasn't a sudden transformation, but a slow refining—through prayer, through quiet mornings in Scripture, and through the kindness of an old family friend, Marion, who reminded me of the basics of faith. I had known about God, but I didn't truly know Him. Over the next few years, He reshaped my rhythms. He taught me to seek His voice before chasing new opportunities. He showed me that the compass doesn't work through striving—it works through surrender.

It wasn't easy. I wrestled with disappointment. I questioned God's timing. But again and again, He whispered, "Your compass still works—let Me show you how to use it."

And here's what I learned: when you give your dreams back to God, He doesn't diminish them; He redeems them. Though I didn't pursue music production the way I once imagined, God opened doors I could never have planned. I found myself working and serving alongside people from different nations and backgrounds, in classrooms, communities, and ministries around the world. He used music in new ways, but He also expanded my perspective far beyond it. What I thought was a detour became a training ground. God was preparing me, refining me, and enlarging my heart to see how He can use every gift, every season, and every man willing to trust His direction.

The compass works through surrender, not striving.

That season taught me more than any classroom or career ever could. It showed me that calling isn't about achievement; it's about alignment. Sometimes, the silence, the delay, and the disappointment are actually God's mercy, pulling you back toward true north. So, if you're in a season that feels uncertain—if your plans have stalled or your sense of direction feels foggy, take heart. You're not off course. You're being refined. Alignment always begins with surrender because before you can walk in purpose, you have to walk with the One who gives it.

According to Barna Group, a leading Christian research organization, one-third of Christian men report feeling real loneliness, even as they long to live with purpose. Many describe unclear rhythms, isolated growth, and a growing disconnect between what they feel called to do and what they feel capable of doing.[2] That gap, between calling and capacity, is where so many men stall out. They know they're meant for more, but they don't know how to bridge the distance. They carry vision without structure, passion without support. And when you're under pressure and alone, that gap becomes paralyzing. But that's exactly where God meets you—not with shame, but with grace, clarity, and tools for realignment. Because His goal isn't just your personal breakthrough. It's to shape your life into a pillar others can lean on. Your obedience, your growth, your consistency—they create space for your family, your brothers, and your community to rise too. That's what becoming more truly means. It's about awakening the man God designed you to be.

If something inside you is flickering right now, that quiet ache for more, that tug toward meaning—don't ignore it. That flicker is sacred. It might be the ache after a long day, or a moment during worship when God whispers that He isn't done with you yet. That flicker isn't failure—it's an

---

[2] Barna group research findings

invitation. The compass still works. It's just waiting for you to pick it up again and to align with it.

When you've wandered long enough, when the noise fades and the striving slows, something begins to settle in you. You start to realize that God was never trying to rush you forward; He was trying to bring you back. Back to stillness. Back to clarity. Back to Him.

When your compass is steady, direction follows. And when your direction is aligned with God, even detours lead to purpose. But how do you begin again? How do you realign after the drift, the resistance, or the years of running on autopilot? You start by learning to use the compass He's already placed inside you.

SPIRITUAL COMPASS FRAMEWORK: ALIGNING YOUR INNER COMPASS

If you've ever felt that tug—the sense that something inside you is meant for more—this is where you begin to rebuild. The compass still works; you just have to learn how to read it again. So, how do you move from drifting to direction? From going through the motions to walking with clarity and purpose? You build your compass, not a physical one, but an internal framework anchored in what matters most. It's a spiritual compass that helps you stay steady when life's winds try to blow you off course. It's a compass with three guiding points:

1. **Faith—Staying Rooted In God's Voice**
   Purpose, without intimacy with God, eventually becomes performance. Your first anchor point must be

your spiritual center. Your compass is clearest when you stay close to God's presence. This isn't about religion—it's about relationship. When you realign your internal compass with God's Word, prayer, and stillness, clarity begins to return.

2. **Brotherhood—Walking With Other Men**

   A compass is most reliable when it's tested in real time—and so is your character. You weren't meant to walk this path alone. You need men who sharpen you, challenge you, and remind you who you are when life's pressure makes you forget. Brotherhood is the grit that keeps you grounded.

3. **Self-Awareness—Knowing When You've Drifted**

   Most men don't crash overnight. They drift. Small decisions, quiet compromises, unspoken fatigue. But when you've built self-awareness into your life—daily reflection, Sabbath rest, check-ins—you begin to notice when your compass is off. Check-ins are regular moments of honest evaluation, either with yourself or with trusted brothers, where you pause and ask hard questions: Am I still aligned with God's patterns? Am I leading with integrity at home? Am I drifting into old patterns? These checkpoints expose small shifts before they become major detours. When you practice them, you course-correct early instead of waiting for the storm.

But awareness alone isn't enough—you need patterns that sustain it. The next section will help you apply rhythms that point you back to presence and purpose.

· ·

Brotherhood is the grit that keeps you grounded.

· ·

LIVING IT OUT: APPLYING YOUR COMPASS

Your compass doesn't demand perfection—it calls for steady alignment. Legacy is shaped in the small, repeatable choices you make each day. Here's how to live it out with intention:

What Are You Planting?

Take five quiet minutes and ask:
- What daily rhythms are shaping the direction of my life right now?
- Are they keeping me aligned with faith, brotherhood, and self-awareness—or pulling me off course?
- What's one way you could rebuild spiritual rhythm this week: prayer, scripture, stillness?

▶ **Who Is Learning From You?**
Identify one person in your life who notices your example.
- How can you model what it looks like to stay rooted in God's voice this week?
- Where can you be honest about your drift, so others see the value of course correction?

▶ **What Truth Anchors Your Compass?**
Choose one scripture to carry with you this week:
- **Proverbs 20:7:** "The righteous lead blameless lives; blessed are their children after them."

- **Galatians 6:9:** "Let us not become weary in doing good, for at the proper time we will reap a harvest if we do not give up."
- **John 15:5:** "I am the vine; you are the branches. If you remain in me and I in you, you will bear much fruit; apart from me you can do nothing."

If you've made it this far, pause and take a breath. You're not here by accident. Something in you still wants more. You may not have it all figured out, but the fact that you're still reading tells me you haven't given up. And that matters.

In this chapter, we've unpacked what it looks like to drift and how to begin returning. We explored the importance of presence, the compass God gives, and the need to anchor in faith, brotherhood, and self-awareness.

But here's the truth: knowing your purpose isn't just about direction; it's about identity. And that's what we'll explore next. When the noise fades and the roles shift, what remains is who you believe you are, and reclaiming who you were always meant to be.

Let's go there.

chapter two

Identity That Can't Be Shaken

There's a moment in every man's life where the spotlight fades, the accolades quiet down, and the inner questions grow louder. When Michael Jordan retired from basketball, he wasn't just stepping off the court—he was stepping into an identity crisis. For years, he was the definition of excellence, competition, and dominance. But after the final buzzer sounded, Jordan later admitted in interviews that he felt lost, wondering who he was apart from the game. He famously said, "I was addicted to the game. It was the only place I could fully express who I was."[3]

And that's the danger many men face—not addiction to basketball, but addiction to performance. We become so accustomed to being defined by what we do, what we build, or how others see us, that when those structures shift or disappear, we're left disoriented.

Michael Jordan's story isn't just about sports—it's about identity, about what happens when external roles no longer define your internal compass. And while your life might not look like his, the question still echoes: Who are you when the

---

[3] Jordan, M., & Vancil, M. (1998). *For the love of the game: My story.* New York, NY: Crown Publishers.

applause stops? When your role changes? When you're not producing results at the pace you once did?

This is when your true identity is tested—not by the applause of the crowd, but by the silence of the soul.

———⊗⊗⊗———

Moving to a new place—especially a new country—has a way of bringing these identity questions to the surface. I've experienced this firsthand. When my family and I moved to Canada, I knew it would be different. I knew it would be colder. I even expected that it would take time to rebuild friendships and reestablish the rhythms of life. But I underestimated just how deeply it would test me.

Your identity is tested in silence, not applause.

In our small rural town, where many people have lived for generations—surrounded by family, childhood friends, and long-standing social circles—being the "new one" felt disorienting. I wasn't just adjusting to a new culture, I was being stripped of the social roots and credibility that once helped define me. When people don't know your story, your work, or your values, it's easy to feel invisible.

What made it even harder was the shift in what I did for work. The kind of community development I had poured myself into wasn't as visible here. The people who once affirmed my contributions weren't around anymore. And even though I had lived and served in several countries before, this season felt different. More hidden. More costly. More internal.

There were mountains of immigration paperwork: countless documents and fees just to secure residency. And moments when I wondered, *why am I doing this? Why not go back to what's familiar?* After a while, I started avoiding telling people where I had come from because they would give me that weird look and a thousand questions as to why I'd moved from Hawaii to Winnipeg, of all places. After a while, even I started wondering why I was truly there.

But deep down, I knew this move wasn't just a relocation. It was a response to God's leading. My wife and I had both sensed it clearly. And even when I miss the palm trees and ocean air of my island upbringing, when friendships are slow to form and identity feels less recognized, I've learned that obedience is worth it. Even when it costs.

What's kept me grounded isn't applause; it's been God's presence, and the handful of friends and family near and far who have reminded me of who I am. Identity isn't always loud. Sometimes, it's built in the quiet decision to stay, to trust, and to keep becoming.

For years I poured myself into community development—leading small ministry teams, building relationships, and launching initiatives. These experiences often brought me deep fulfillment, but behind the scenes, I often tied my worth to visibility, outcomes, and perceived impact. I thought I was serving from purpose, but at times I was striving for affirmation. That's when I began learning what it means to build an identity that can't be shaken—not in titles, not in metrics, but in the quiet work of becoming—because God isn't just interested in what we build; He's forming who we are as we build it.

This isn't just a chapter about identity—it's a turning point in your journey. Because, if your foundation isn't rooted in who you are in Christ, everything you build will eventually collapse under the weight of what others expect.

> **God isn't just interested in what we build;**
> **He's forming who we are as we build it.**

Scripture shows us again and again that God forms identity in the hidden place long before He reveals it on a platform. David was anointed king while still watching sheep, years before he ever held a crown (1 Samuel 16). Joseph endured betrayal, slavery, and prison before stepping into influence in Pharaoh's court (Genesis 37–41). Even Jesus spent thirty silent years in obscurity before beginning His public ministry (Luke 2:51–52, Luke 3:23). Their stories remind us that the hidden place isn't punishment; it's preparation. It's where God refines a man's heart before entrusting him with greater influence.

Maybe you're in that kind of season right now, where the spotlight has faded, the role has shifted, or the affirmation has gone quiet. And in that quiet, you've started to feel the tension: *Who am I now?* That's not failure. That's formation. Identity work doesn't begin when you're finally seen, it begins when you choose to let God rebuild what no one else sees—not the platform, but the man standing on it.

THE COUNTERFEIT IDENTITIES MEN CARRY

Every man has wrestled with the weight of false identities—those invisible roles and labels we pick up along the way. Some we inherited. Some we built. Some were placed on us by others.

There's the **Provider Identity**—where your worth is tied to how much you earn or how well you provide for your family. The **Performer Identity**—where you believe you're only valuable when you're producing, achieving, or outperforming everyone else. The **Protector Identity**—where your masculinity is measured by how much danger you can prevent or pain you can endure without showing weakness. The **Position Identity**—where your significance is tied to a title, role, or level of influence. The **Problem-Solver Identity**—where you feel like a failure anytime you can't fix something quickly or perfectly.

None of these identities are inherently wrong—being a provider, protector, or problem-solver are good things. But when they become the *core of your identity*, rather than expressions of your purpose, they start to distort how you see yourself.

As author Brené Brown puts it: "When you tie your self-worth to your productivity, you're one setback away from a shame spiral."[4] That's the risk of performance-based identity—it's always one failure away from collapse. It's like building a house on scaffolding instead of a foundation—it may look solid for a while, but it won't last when pressure hits.

Here's the deeper issue: when our identity is unstable, our leadership becomes performative. We become driven by comparison, consumed by what others think, and constantly exhausted from trying to hold it all together. But the truth is this: you weren't made to carry a manufactured identity. You were created to live from a secure one, anchored in Christ, not applause, and rooted in sonship, not status.

So, what identity have you been quietly carrying that isn't rooted in who God says you are? You're not the first man to wrestle with this. In fact, some of the most powerful men in Scripture walked through identity storms before stepping into their calling.

David was anointed as king long before he wore the crown. Before anyone saw him as royalty, he was a shepherd boy—tending sheep, playing music, and fighting lions in the unseen fields. His identity wasn't forged in the throne room; it was refined in the pasture. Even after his anointing, he faced rejection, betrayal, and years of hiding in caves. But it was in those hidden places that his character was shaped, his faith deepened, and his identity secured, not by applause, but by intimacy with God.

---

[4] Brown, B. (2010). The gifts of imperfection: Let go of who you think you're supposed to be and embrace who you are. Center City, MN: Hazelden.

Moses was called to lead a nation, but he first spent forty years in the wilderness. After fleeing Egypt, he lived in obscurity, tending sheep in a place far from the platforms of Pharaoh's court. He went from power to exile, from recognition to stillness. But it was in the wilderness that Moses encountered God in the burning bush, and he discovered that identity wasn't found in titles or influence but in obedience and relationship.

Peter was bold, passionate, and impulsive, but also deeply insecure. He pledged loyalty to Jesus but failed when it mattered most. And yet, after his denial, Jesus didn't disqualify Peter, instead He restored him. In a quiet conversation over breakfast, Jesus reminded Peter of who he truly was and what he was called to do. Peter's identity wasn't built on perfection—it was rebuilt through grace.

These men weren't shaped in moments of glory—they were forged in seasons of obscurity, failure, and waiting. But their identity became solid because they allowed God to define them, not their title, their past, or their performance.

And that's the invitation for every man reading this: not to perfect yourself, but to surrender to the process of becoming. You won't get it all right overnight, but that's not the point. The goal isn't perfection. It's formation. Let God strip away what's false so He can strengthen what's real.

So how do you start building an identity that actually lasts, one that won't collapse under pressure, success, or failure? Let's walk through it together.

HOW TO BUILD IDENTITY THAT LASTS

Building a lasting identity isn't about performing harder or projecting confidence. It's about anchoring yourself to something deeper, something unshakable when everything else gets tested.

You don't build a stable identity on public success; you build it on private surrender. It starts with presence: the consistent rhythm of being with God—not just working for Him. Your identity deepens every time you show up in silence, in scripture, in brotherhood—not for applause, but for alignment.

It's built through obedience, not outcome. Identity rooted in Christ comes from trusting Him in the small, hidden assignments. Every step of faith in the unseen strengthens your internal compass.

You don't build a stable identity on public success; you build it on private surrender.

You don't have to become someone else; you need to remember who you already are. This identity isn't earned but inherited. As sons of God, we don't achieve our place in His family by performance; we receive it by adoption through Christ. Scripture makes this clear: "the Spirit you received brought about your adoption to sonship. And by him we cry, 'Abba, Father'" (Romans 8:15). Our identity is not a reward for good behavior but a gift of grace, secured by what Jesus has already done. Paul reminds us in Galatians 4:7, "So you are no longer a slave, but God's child; and since you are his child, God has made you also an heir."

That's what it means to have an inherited identity; it's passed down from the Father, confirmed through the Son, and sealed by the Spirit. It's a gift from being in His presence and not the result of your effort. Then it is solidified in community. And with an identity that is grounded in truth, when life shakes the surface, your roots will hold.

So, if you've ever felt like you're hustling for worth or chasing applause just to feel valuable, pause. That's not where your identity comes from. The world will try to label you by what you do, what you earn, or how much you can carry. But God's been speaking a better name over you since the beginning: son.

Think of identity as calibration. Before you follow your compass into calling, you need clarity about who you are. Because, without identity, even the right assignment will feel like a burden. But when your inner world is anchored, when you stop performing for worth and start living from it, you begin to move with courage, not confusion.

Leadership author John Maxwell once said, "Success is when I add value to myself. Significance is when I add value to others."[5] That's the difference between striving and serving, between living from a false identity and walking in a secure one.

---

[5] Maxwell, J. C. (2015). *Intentional living: Choosing a life that matters.* New York, NY: Center Street.

Don't rush past this chapter. Sit with it. Wrestle with it. Let God speak to the core of who you are, not just as a man, but as a son. Because that's your compass. That's your true north.

And as you turn the page, the journey goes deeper. Because once you begin to rebuild identity in Christ, you'll start confronting the beliefs that tried to define you in the first place. If your identity doesn't come from God, it's coming from somewhere, and usually, that "somewhere" is a mix of past wounds, inherited mindsets, and internal narratives that need to be dismantled.

So, get ready to break the ceilings you didn't even know you were living under.

Let's keep climbing.

LIVING IT OUT: BECOMING THE MAN WITHIN

Identity isn't built on recognition—it's forged in the quiet places where you discover who you are apart from performance and establish spiritual anchors. These simple practices help move identity from head knowledge to heart transformation:

- **Start your day in stillness.** Before the world starts shouting, take a few moments to simply be with God.
- **Pray this:** "God, remind me who I am, before the world tells me otherwise."
- **Wait.** Don't rush past that moment. Sit in stillness. Listen for what He whispers about you. Write it down.

▶ **What Are You Planting?**

Take five quiet minutes and ask:

- Where am I relying on performance or titles to define me?
- What habits or choices are strengthening my identity in Christ?

▶ **Who Is Learning From You?**

Identity is modeled as much as it is taught.

- Who in your life is watching how you navigate hidden seasons or unseen work?
- How can you model patience, obedience, and trust in God's timing for them this week?

▶ **What Truth Anchors Your Identity?**

Carry one of these scriptures with you as a reminder that your worth isn't tied to performance, but to your identity as God's son:

- **1 John 3:1** "See what great love the Father has lavished on us, that we should be called children of God! And that is what we are!"
- **Romans 8:16** "The Spirit himself testifies with our spirit that we are God's children."
- **1 Peter 2:9** "But you are a chosen people, a royal priesthood, a holy nation, God's special possession, that you may declare the praises of him who called you out of darkness into his wonderful light."

chapter three

Breaking the Inner Ceiling: Confronting the Beliefs That Hold You Back

Sometimes it's not a wall in front of you that stops your momentum, it's the invisible ceiling above you that you've never questioned. Most men don't realize they're living under a ceiling until something in their spirit starts asking, "Why do I keep hitting the same wall?"

The internal limitations are the unspoken narratives, inherited mindsets, and self-imposed ceilings that quietly shape how we live, lead, love, and relate to God. And over time, these hidden ceilings don't just limit what we believe is possible—they begin to inform who we believe we are. They write false-identity scripts that sound familiar: I'm only valuable when I'm producing; I'm only a man if I'm protecting or providing; I can't show weakness; I have to fix it. These aren't just lies, they're echoes of the very identities we began naming in the last chapter: the Performer, the Provider, the Problem-Solver. And unless we confront these beliefs, they quietly become the foundation we build our lives on.

Every man wrestles with internal beliefs. Some are formed by past wounds. Others are passed down through generations. And some were etched into us through failure, silence, or shame.

It's one thing to have a calling—it's another to believe you're worthy of carrying it. And until you confront the beliefs buried beneath your habits, you'll keep living from a version of yourself that God never intended. As Proverbs 23:7 (KJV) reminds us, "As a man thinks in his heart, so is he."

WHERE LIMITING BELIEFS BEGIN

I didn't grow up in a home without love. In fact, I had a great father. He was consistent, responsible, and deeply committed to our family. He ran a family business and was always working—designing machines, building things, and managing multiple projects. His work ethic shaped a lot of how I understood manhood. He was a provider, a problem-solver, and a man who carried responsibility with quiet strength.

But what I didn't always see was emotional vulnerability. My dad didn't talk much about how he felt, and affection didn't come easily—yes, he was humorous and would tell jokes at times, but the emotional distance, the quiet when it came to how he really felt, started to make more sense as I got older. I came to realize that much of that silence was shaped by his own story. He had lost his father at fifteen. Loss like this doesn't just create grief—it creates ceilings. When you lose that kind of safety early on, vulnerability can feel risky; opening up can start to feel dangerous. So instead of expressing pain, you learn to stay strong. You bury what hurts. You keep moving. And survival, while necessary, often builds walls where there should have been bridges.

For me growing up, I didn't often see vulnerability modeled—not in him, and not in his relationship with my mom either. Even when conflict happened in front of us as kids, I rarely saw apologies or emotional repair. Without even realizing it, I picked up some of my father's ceilings—not because he had failed, but because he had modeled strength without softness, work without rest, areas of responsibility without emotional depth.

> ## Survival, while necessary, often builds walls where bridges should exist.

I remember the day I got the phone call. I was on a golf course with a friend—refreshing some basics and enjoying a casual round—when my sister called. I didn't expect that moment to shift everything. She told me my father had been hospitalized. It was serious. And everything in me knew I needed to get home.

I booked the first available flight to Jamaica. But it was too late; by the time I arrived, he was gone. Interestingly, while I awaited my connecting flight at Toronto Pearson Airport, I met an Israeli guy in his late twenties who shared with me about some of his challenges with his dad and how he wished his father could understand him more. Little did he know that as he spoke, I was losing my own father. I found myself in a unique position to share on a topic that was at the moment, painful, and yet at the same time felt like I had some good words to offer. I encouraged him that he should do all he could to make amends.

I still remember sitting on the plane, staring out the window, unsure if I was too late, unsure if I had said enough to my dad. My sister had told me it was serious, and though I didn't have confirmation yet, something in me feared the worst. That flight was quiet, but inside me, everything was loud. I was bracing for what I might walk into. And in the stillness, memories started flooding in. I was afraid I'd lost him and I was already remembering him. Mourning, in a way, had already begun in my spirit. I remembered how he used to take me and my siblings jogging at the beach on early weekend mornings— the waves crashing on the seashore, the cool ocean breeze, our laughter as we swam, and the joy of discovering seashells we'd bring home for our collection. He believed strongly in physical health and often reminded us that what we put in our bodies impacted our longevity and overall quality of life. I remembered evenings visiting at our business place—how some of the workers would affectionately say, "Bailey's son is here, man", when they saw me coming through the door after school. There was a kind of pride knowing my dad was the owner, and in a way, me too. I'd try to sneak into his back office and scare him, but it rarely worked. He'd always catch me with that knowing smile.

Those memories stayed with me on that flight, and long after. But so did the silence, the things he never said, the emotions he never expressed. I wasn't just mourning my father—I was confronting everything he passed down to me—his legacy, his values, his quiet way of carrying life, and the limitations I had unknowingly inherited too.

That's the thing about belief systems, they're not always loud. Some of the strongest ceilings in a man's life are formed in silence, in what was modeled but never named, and in what was present, but never processed. And unless you stop to examine the ceilings you've internalized, you'll keep living beneath them, thinking it's just how life works. Some of the internal scripts I'd never questioned had begun to rise to the surface, beliefs like "being a man means holding it all together," or "if I slow down, I'll let people down."

Somewhere along the way, I realized I was starting to repeat some of those same silent patterns with my own kids—not intentionally, just unconsciously. It wasn't that I was repeating everything from my upbringing, but that the silence I grew up with could've easily shown up again. It would've been easy to focus only on providing or protecting—to stay busy, to let "being present" mean physically showing up, but emotionally staying guarded. I had to face those ceilings head-on; I didn't want to pass them down.

But I realized how hard it was to model something I had never really seen. How do you extend what was never demonstrated? How do you give language to emotions you were never taught to name? Because I hadn't seen it in my father, I knew I needed to be intentional. I leaned into more dialogue with my wife so I could learn from her, and I invested in marriage books, training seminars, and spaces where I could grow in the areas I hadn't inherited. What I didn't receive by example, I chose to pursue by practice. I started asking deeper questions about identity, presence, and emotional health, not just for my family's sake, but for my own.

By God's grace, I've made it a point to say the things I didn't hear growing up. I tell my sons I love them. I make space for their emotions. I let them see me wrestle, pray, and reflect. I'm still learning, but I'm not leading from silence anymore.

This is what breaking generational patterns looks like: not perfection, but presence. Not pretending you've got it all figured out, but inviting the Holy Spirit into the gaps your father couldn't fill.

What I lacked by example, I pursued through practice.

Grief has a way of pulling things out of hiding—questions, memories, unfinished conversations. But it also becomes a mirror. It shows you not just what you lost, but what you've carried unknowingly for years.

Limiting beliefs don't just appear out of nowhere, as I have demonstrated from my journey. They're formed in the background of our stories—through wounds, whispers, silence, culture, and upbringing. They often begin long before we're aware they exist.

Some come from childhood through words spoken (or not spoken) over us. Or they enter through environments where performance was rewarded but vulnerability was ignored. Others are absorbed through culture—the pressure to be successful, emotionless, untouchable.

Still others are passed down generationally—family belief systems wrapped in survival, fear, or pride.

Maybe you grew up hearing:

- "Real men don't cry."
- "You have to earn your worth."
- "If you're not strong, you're a failure."
- "Keep your emotions to yourself."
- "Don't dream too big—it's not for people like us."

Even if you have never heard these phrases directly, you may have felt them in the air around you—through silence, body language, expectations, or patterns that repeated without being challenged.

Limiting beliefs don't always sound like lies—they often sound like wisdom, and that's what makes them dangerous. They blend in. They feel familiar. And over time, they become frameworks for how we view ourselves, others, and even God.

These beliefs don't just distort how we see ourselves—they often distort how we see God. We start believing He's distant, demanding, or disappointed—when in truth, He's a father who speaks identity, not shame.

Just because something feels true doesn't mean it is.

Until you expose the root of these beliefs, you'll keep living with spiritual ceilings that God never placed over you. And the only way to break them is to bring them into the light—name them, challenge them, and replace them with truth. This is where the real work of transformation starts.

→ **What beliefs have shaped how I view myself and which of them need to be unlearned?**

If this section stirred something in you, take heart. You're not weak for wrestling with these things—you're wise. It takes courage to name what's been buried, and strength to begin realigning your inner life with God's truth.

This isn't about perfection—it's about progression. You don't have to rewrite every belief overnight. You just need to begin replacing the false narrative one truth at a time.

BREAKING THE INNER CEILING: NAMING THE LIE

Transformation begins when truth replaces the lie. Every internal ceiling is held up by a belief system, and the only way to dismantle it is to identify what's been holding it up in the first place. This process isn't complicated, but it is courageous. It takes spiritual honesty to pause long enough to ask, "What's the lie I've been believing, and what's the truth God wants me to build my life upon instead?"

Here's a simple framework to help you begin:

1. **Name the Lie:** What is the core limiting belief that keeps replaying in your mind? It may sound like:
   - "I'm not enough."
   - "I have to prove myself to be valuable."
   - "I'm too broken to lead."
   - "I always mess it up."
   - "I can't trust anyone."

Don't just glance over it—say it out loud. Write it down. Bring it into the light. Don't be surprised if this process stirs emotion—it means you're healing. Truth always meets us in tender places.

And don't try to do this alone—ask the Holy Spirit to help you uncover the roots and guide you into truth. He's not just a comforter—He's a revealer. Sometimes you'll need a brother to help you name the lie and speak truth when your own voice feels weak.

2. **Trace the Source:** Where did the belief begin? Was it a conversation, a wound, a repeated experience, or something modeled to you? Sometimes identifying the origin helps disempower the illusion of truth.

3. **Challenge the Agreement:** In other words, have you been silently agreeing with this lie without realizing it? If so, now's the moment to renounce it. You don't have to carry that script any longer.

4. **Replace it with Truth:** Ask the Holy Spirit to lead you to a scripture-based truth that dismantles the lie. He's the revealer—and He knows exactly what your heart needs to hear. When He highlights a verse, hold on to it. Speak it aloud. Write it where you'll see it often. Let Him confront the lie, reshape your thinking, and remind you who you really are.

As Romans 12:2 declares: "Do not conform to the pattern of this world but be transformed by the renewing of your mind. Then you will be able to test and approve what God's will is—His good, pleasing and perfect will."

This isn't a one-time journal moment—it's a habit of transformation. The more you practice replacing lies with truth, the more your mind and heart begin to align with heaven's perspective.

- **Lie:** "I always mess it up."
- **Truth:** "My grace is sufficient for you, for my power is made perfect in weakness." (2 Corinthians 12:9).
- **Lie:** "I'm not enough."
- **Truth:** "For we are God's handiwork, created in Christ Jesus to do good works, which God prepared in advance for us to do." (Ephesians 2:10).

This is how inner ceilings break—not with noise, but with clarity. Not through striving, but through surrender to truth.

Replacing lies with truth aligns your heart and mind.

As you begin to replace lies with truth, you're not just removing ceilings—you're rising into your God-given identity. You're not becoming someone new—you're becoming who you've always been in Christ.

You cannot build a new identity on an old belief system. That's why replacing the lie isn't the end of the work; it's the beginning of renewal and it's ongoing. It's not a motivational boost—it's spiritual formation. When the false narrative is removed, it must be replaced with truth that is rooted in God's Word, God's voice, and God's heart for you.

And here's the truth:

You are not what happened to you. **You are not** what you failed at. **You are not** the words others spoke over you. **You are not** the sum of your insecurities, your past, or your performance.

You are who God says you are. You are His son. **You are** chosen. **You are** forgiven. **You are** equipped. **You are** called. **You are** strong in Him. **You are** full of purpose, even when you feel unsure. **You are** anchored in grace, even when your past whispers shame. **You are** more than a man trying to measure up—you are a man who's been raised up in Christ.

Truth isn't just informational; it's transformational. Truth doesn't transform you just because you read it—it transforms you when you begin to believe it, rehearse it, and live from it. The more you meditate on who you are in Christ, the more you begin to live from that place rather than striving to earn it.

Don't just read the identity truths listed above—say them out loud. Speak them over yourself. Let your voice become a mirror of heaven's truth about who you are.

This is the journey of becoming who you've always been in the heart of God.

⁘

As you begin replacing lies with truth, you'll feel something shift inside you, not always loud or dramatic, but steady and real. That's the power of clarity. But clarity doesn't erase the weight. In fact, sometimes it makes you more aware of it. Now that you're walking in a new identity, the pressure to hold it all together can feel even heavier. You start noticing the weight of expectations, responsibilities, and silent burdens you've been carrying for years. But here's the good news: you don't have to carry it alone. In the next chapter, we'll unpack what that weight really is, where it comes from, and how to discern what's yours to carry, and what's not. Because when you learn to release what God never asked you to hold, you make room to walk lighter, lead better, and live freer.

Release what God never asked you to carry.

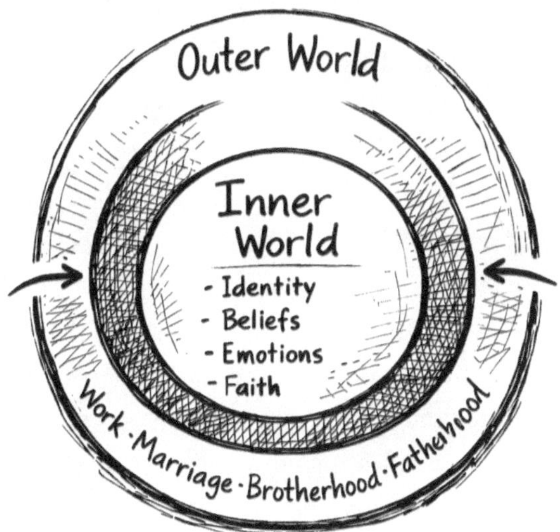
Inner vs Outer Battle
Outer World
Inner
World
- Identity
- Beliefs
- Emotions
- Faith
Work · Marriage · Brotherhood · Fatherhood

LIVING IT OUT: BREAKING INNER CEILINGS

False ceilings aren't just obstacles, they're invitations to deeper identity. Here are three ways to start breaking them this week:

► **Where Am I Still Living Small?**
Take ten minutes this week to reflect or journal:
- What belief has been holding me back?
- What truth is God inviting me to live from instead?

► **Who's Reminding Me Who I Am?**
Reach out to one brother or mentor.
- Share one lie you've been carrying and one truth you're choosing to walk in.

► **What Truth Will Anchor Me This Week?**
Choose one verse to declare daily:
- **Romans 12:2** "Do not conform to the pattern of this world, but be transformed by the renewing of your mind. Then you will be able to test and approve what God's will is—his good, pleasing and perfect will."
- **Ephesians 2:10** "For we are God's handiwork, created in Christ Jesus to do good works, which God prepared in advance for us to do."
- **Galatians 2:20** "I have been crucified with Christ and I no longer live, but Christ lives in me. The life I now live in the body, I live by faith in the Son of God, who loved me and gave himself for me."

chapter four

The Weight You Carry: Understanding the Pressures That Shape You

Every man carries weight: the weight of responsibility, the weight of provision, the weight of unspoken expectations, and the pressure to be enough, to hold it all together and still stay strong. Some of it you were assigned, and some you picked up along the way. If you're honest, you might not even know where it came from—you just know you feel it every day. No one told you it would feel this heavy. No one explained how invisible pressure could be just as exhausting as visible work. And most of the time, you don't even have the language for it—you just push through, numb up, or press on.

But what if the pressure you carry isn't just a burden—it's also a teacher? What if it's revealing something deeper about how you see yourself, how you see God, and how you've been conditioned to perform instead of rest?

As Jesus reminded us, "Come to me, all you who are weary and burdened, and I will give you rest" (Matthew 11:28). The challenge is learning to discern which weights are from God and which ones you were never meant to carry, and most of all, learning how to exchange pressure for peace without losing purpose.

Pressure piles on slowly, until one day you're not sure if you're leading from purpose or just driven by pressure. Most men know exactly what that feels like. Pressure doesn't just come in one form—it shows up everywhere:

- **Work Pressure**—The weight of performance, deadlines, expectations, and the fear of not measuring up.
- **Family Pressure**—The desire to provide, protect, lead, and nurture, even when you feel unsure or tired yourself.
- **Spiritual Pressure** —The expectation to stay spiritually strong, to never waver, to keep showing up for others while secretly needing support yourself.
- **Cultural Pressure**—The constant noise that tells you you're not enough unless you have more, do more, or achieve more.

Sometimes it's not even pressure from others, but it's the pressure we put on ourselves. The silent inner voice that says: "Don't slow down. Don't drop the ball. Don't let anyone see you struggle."

Even biblical leaders felt it. Moses, when called to lead, responded with fear and hesitation (Exodus 3–4). He carried the pressure of guiding a nation while feeling unqualified. Elijah, after defeating the prophets of Baal, crumbled under emotional exhaustion and isolation (1 Kings 19). David, after gaining the crown, still carried the invisible weight of his internal battles and brokenness (Psalm 32; 2 Samuel 11–12).

Their stories remind us that even those anointed by God felt the tension between calling and capacity. So, if you've ever felt that tension too, if you've carried a weight you couldn't name, or a pressure that didn't let up, it's not because you're weak. It's because you were never meant to carry it all alone. The pressure you feel isn't proof of failure. It's a reminder of your need for grace, strength beyond your own, and a rhythm that includes rest. I started to learn this in an ordinary moment with my family.

HOW PRESSURE SHOWS UP IN A MAN'S LIFE

I remember a moment during a trip to Vancouver Island with my wife and our two boys. We had set out to enjoy a few days away as a family—to disconnect, rest, reset and celebrate our tenth anniversary. One afternoon, while exploring a local trail, we came across a small blacksmith shop tucked beside the path. Inside, the blacksmith was heating metal in the fire, hammering and shaping it with rhythmic precision.

My boys Kalino and Kawika were captivated. Their eyes wide with wonder, they asked, "Daddy, why does he keep putting it back in the fire?"

I knelt beside them and explained: "He's not burning it to destroy it—he's strengthening it. The fire makes the metal flexible, so it can be shaped. But if it never goes through the fire, it stays brittle. It won't hold anything under pressure." Or something along that line and of course, they had way more questions that followed.

As I spoke, I realized I wasn't just teaching them a lesson about metal: I was preaching to myself. In fact, I was revisiting a truth I'd seen play out again and again in my own life.

That image stayed with me, because life often feels like a furnace. And sometimes what you're going through isn't punishment—it's purpose. God doesn't place you in the fire to break you—but to forge you.

Later that evening, I reflected on a different kind of fire, one I walked through in 2012. It was a season of pressure that shook almost every area of my life. At the time, I was a young leader, full of passion and vision. I had been entrusted with real responsibility, and I didn't take that lightly. When my leaders cast vision, I ran with it. I executed. I got results. That's how I was wired: make it happen, solve the problem, and keep things moving. And for a while, that worked. Projects were completed, goals were met, momentum was building, and everything seemed on track. I was passionate, but I wasn't being mentored. At one point, while I thought I was solving a problem and helping things move forward, I overstepped my responsibility and made a call without checking in with the proper authority. While my heart was in the right place, I had moved too fast, and it was decided that I needed to step back from my role. And while part of me wrestled with how it all unfolded—if the consequences matched the action—I didn't resist. I didn't try to defend myself. Because even if the situation didn't fully validate the decision, I now know the decision validated a deeper work God wanted to do in me. I could feel the Holy Spirit whispering, "Let this season refine you."

. . . .

God doesn't place you in the fire to break you— but to forge you.

. . . .

That transition triggered a wave of internal pressure. I had a deep desire to lead—but now, I was flooded with uncertainty. I felt emotionally stretched, mentally fatigued, and somewhat spiritually disoriented. I began to wonder was I ever really ready? Did I just ruin everything God had placed in my hands?

But I didn't run. I didn't quit. I stayed. I listened. I let the correction become construction.

And in that sacred stretch, something unexpected happened. That very season opened new doors for me to meet some of my best mentors—men I had been searching for but didn't know existed. They helped me understand my wiring, my blind spots, and what healthy leadership truly requires. That season, in many ways, was a blessing in disguise.

Looking back, I now see it not as punishment, but as preparation. That fire didn't destroy me. It refined me. It carved something deeper into my character that I wouldn't have developed any other way: patience, humility, discernment, a hunger for mentorship, and a much clearer sense that leadership isn't just about momentum, it's about maturity.

In fact, that experience is one of the reasons I've invested so deeply in my work as a life coach. I believe every man needs people who will walk with him, not just to affirm his gifts, but to refine them. We grow not just through success, but through pressure, through correction, and through clarity.

Just like the blacksmith we saw that day, heating and reshaping metal through repeated fire and force—God was doing the same with me.

It wasn't the fire I wanted. But it was the fire I needed. And I'm grateful for it.

NOT ALL PRESSURE IS EQUAL

Pressure has a way of revealing what's underneath. After that season, I began to notice something: I wasn't the only one walking through fire. Every man I talked to, whether a pastor, entrepreneur, father, or friend, was carrying something. Stress. Doubt. Exhaustion. A fear of not being enough. Most of it wasn't loud. But all of it was heavy.

And the weight wasn't always coming from the same place. That's what makes pressure so complex. It comes in layers. Some is inherited, expectations passed down from family systems. Some is internal, formed by our own insecurities and unspoken fears. Some is cultural, driven by the pressure to hustle, succeed, and never appear weak. And some is spiritual, birthed from the tension of carrying God's call without always feeling God's strength. This is why we need discernment, because not all pressure is created equal.

Jesus tells a story in Matthew 7 about two builders. One built on sand: easy, quick, comfortable. The other built on rock: slower, harder, but secure. Then came the storm.

Both builders faced the same wind, rain, and flood, but only one house stood.

Jesus wasn't just talking about building houses. He was talking about building lives.

Storms don't always introduce new problems. Sometimes they just expose the ones that are already there. Pressure will test whether your life is built on convenience or conviction, or whether you've been following God out of rhythm or out of relationship. It reveals whether you've been quoting scripture or living it.

And it begs the question: What kind of pressure are you facing right now? Not all storms are the same. Some are meant to redirect you. Others are meant to refine you.

TWO TYPES OF STORMS: JONAH'S CRISIS VS. JOB'S CRISIS

Not every storm in your life is the same. Some storms come from our disobedience. Others come from God's permission. And how you navigate pressure depends on understanding what kind of storm you're actually in.

Let's look at two men from Scripture, Jonah and Job. Both experienced intense pressure. But the reasons, and the results, were very different.

Jonah's storm was self-inflicted. God gave him a clear assignment: go to Nineveh. Jonah refused and went the opposite direction. The storm that followed wasn't random, it was correction, a divine disruption meant to realign him with his purpose.

That storm wasn't punishment; it was mercy. God used the chaos to awaken Jonah to what he was running from. And sometimes, God will shake the boat not to destroy you, but to wake you up.

If you're in a Jonah-type storm, the most courageous thing you can do isn't to fight harder, it's to surrender—to stop carrying a calling in a direction it was never meant to go. You don't fight your way out of disobedience, you repent your way forward.

But not all storms come from rebellion. **Job's storm was different.** In the Old Testament book of Job, we're told that Job was a man of integrity—blameless, upright, and deeply devoted to God. And yet, his life was turned upside down. He lost his family, his health, his livelihood, through no fault of his own. Why? Because God trusted him. Job's storm wasn't about correction; it was about revelation. A deeper encounter with God was on the other side of his suffering. His pressure didn't expose sin, it revealed depth. Job said it himself near the end of his story: "My ears had heard of you, but now my eyes have seen you" (Job 42:5). His storm stripped everything external so that something internal could be formed.

Whether your storm is like Jonah's or Job's, the refining purpose of God can still be at work. One storm redirects you. The other deepens you. Both transform you, if you let them.

The kind of storm you're in shapes the kind of resilience you'll need. Some storms call you to surrender and reroute. Others call you to stand still and go deeper. But all storms, whether born of rebellion or refinement, can lead to transformation when you allow God to work in you through them.

So, ask yourself: **What kind of storm am I in?**

WHAT RESILIENCE REALLY LOOKS LIKE— STRENGTH IN THE VALLEY

Often, I hear people say, "resilience is about having a thick skin", but I believe it's more than that—it's about having a deep well. It's not just about pushing through pain—it's about drawing strength from something deeper when your own capacity runs out.

Too often, men confuse resilience with stoicism. Keep your head down. Tough it out. Don't show weakness. But biblical resilience isn't about hiding your pain; it's about anchoring your heart to God's truth—not to your feelings, not to your outcomes—but to the steady, unchanging presence of a God who doesn't shift when your world does.

David, the warrior-king, wrote in Psalm 23, "Even though I walk through the valley of the shadow of death, I will fear no evil, for You are with me." That's not the voice of a man pretending everything's fine. That's the voice of a man who knows where his strength truly comes from.

The world tells you to perform your way out of pain. But God invites you to persevere your way through it. It's not always glamorous. It's often quiet, but it's powerful. Hebrews 10:36 reminds us, "You need to persevere so that when you have done the will of God, you will receive what he has promised."

So how do you build resilience as a man of faith? It starts from the inside out.

- **Keep Showing Up** (Purposeful Habits)—Resilience is built in small daily rhythms, not grand declarations.

Things like waking early to pray, journaling your thoughts, or setting boundaries on work help you stay rooted.

- **Speak Honestly with God** (Emotional Honesty)—Don't filter your prayers. God can handle your frustration, your doubt, your fatigue. Pretending doesn't strengthen you, truth does.
- **Filter what Forms You** (Spiritual Anchoring)—What you consume shapes your soul. Scripture, worship, and wise counsel all reinforce your foundation when life shakes you.
- **Invest in Rest**—Resilient men know when to pause. Sabbath isn't weakness; it's wisdom. You're not a machine. You're a vessel. Rest helps you refill.
- **Check Your Compass often**—Revisit your spiritual alignment regularly. Drift is subtle, but real. Don't wait until you're lost to recalibrate.

Resilience isn't about being invincible; it's about being rooted. It's not about having it all together, but about knowing where to go when you don't.

RESILIENCE IN REAL LIFE: WHAT IT LOOKS LIKE WHERE YOU ARE

Resilience is not something you practice in isolation; it shows up in the way you move through your daily life. Use the space below to reflect on how God is forming strength in you across each of these areas:

- **At Work:** Resilience looks like showing up with integrity even when you're unrecognized. It's keeping your composure when everything's urgent and chaotic, and refusing to cut corners just to keep up. It's choosing peace over pressure and character over image, even when promotion seems slow.
  Reflection: What challenge am I currently facing that is testing my character or patience?

- **In Marriage:** Resilience looks like listening when you'd rather defend. It's staying emotionally present when you feel distant. It's choosing grace over withdrawal—like choosing to ask your wife how she's really doing, even when you're tired or frustrated. It's saying "I'm sorry" first, even if part of you wants to shut down or walk away. It's leaning in instead of shutting down and committing to love when the feelings fluctuate. It's showing up with humility, not perfection.
  Reflection: What's one unspoken pressure I need to acknowledge and talk about with my spouse?

- **In Parenting:** Resilience looks like patience when your children test your limits. It's consistency when life is unpredictable. It's modelling prayer when you're tired, and discipline when you'd rather retreat. It's creating space to nurture, not just manage, the souls in your home.
  Reflection: This week, what's one way I can slow down and truly connect with my child, without

rushing, correcting, or multitasking? What does parenting from presence, not pressure, look like in this season?

- **In Brotherhood and Friendship:** Resilience looks like vulnerability when culture tells you to isolate. It's sending that text, making that call, initiating that conversation—not because you feel strong, but because you refuse to walk alone. Brotherhood is forged when you're honest, not polished.

  Reflection: Where have I held back emotionally, and what would it take to be more honest?

- **In Leadership or Ministry:** Resilience looks like serving when applause is absent. It's leading with compassion when criticism stings. It's keeping boundaries when burnout is creeping in. It's staying faithful to God's voice even when results don't come fast.

  Reflection: Am I measuring my leadership by outcomes… or obedience?

  o   Am I leading to impress, or to serve?

  o   Where do I need to pause, refocus, and realign with God's purpose—not just people's expectations?

⸺⸺∞⸺⸺

> ## Resilience isn't about having it all together but knowing where to go when you don't.

The truth is every man will carry weight. The question isn't whether pressure will come, it's whether you'll have the resilience to withstand it. Without resilience, pressure eventually crushes you, leaving you burned out, bitter, or broken. But with resilience, anchored in God's presence, shaped through practice, and strengthened in brotherhood, the same pressure that once felt unbearable can become the very fire that forges your character.

Resilience doesn't remove the weight, but it gives you the strength to carry it without being crushed by it. And when the pressure feels heavier than your strength, prayer becomes the place where resilience is renewed. That's where we turn next—into the mystery of silence, where God often deepens men not through striving, but through His steady presence.

LIVING IT OUT: BUILDING RESILIENCE THAT LASTS

Resilience doesn't happen by accident. It's formed through daily choices, honest reflection, and spiritual anchoring. Here are three ways to apply what you've just read:

▶ **Where Am I Carrying Pressure God Never Asked Me To?**

Take ten minutes this week to reflect or journal: What expectations, demands, or silent burdens have I taken on that God didn't place on my shoulders? What would it look like to surrender them?

▶ **Who Knows What I'm Really Carrying?**

Resilience isn't isolation, it's forged in brotherhood. This week, talk with one trusted friend. Share one place you feel weary, and one place you're growing.

▶ **What's One Scripture I Can Anchor To This Week?**

Pick one and let it guide how you respond to pressure:

- **Matthew 11:28** "Come to me, all you who are weary and burdened, and I will give you rest."
- **Psalm 23:4** "Even though I walk through the darkest valley, I will fear no evil, for you are with me; your rod and your staff, they comfort me."

- **Hebrews 10:36** "You need to persevere so that when you have done the will of God, you will receive what he has promised."

DECLARATION

Finish this sentence: "This week, I will _________________ ________________________________, because I believe God is forming strength in me that will last."

Remember, resilience is forged, not found. It's not about being invincible. It's about being rooted, consistent, and anchored in who God says you are.

chapter five

Praying Through the Silence: When God Feels Distant

There are seasons when heaven feels quiet. Not because God has left, but because He's doing something deeper than what we can hear, see, or feel in the moment. Even after we confront the lies and begin to walk in truth, there are still seasons where God's voice feels quiet and our hearts feel uncertain. Silence, for many men, isn't just frustrating—it's disorienting. Sometimes it's not the silence that hurts the most—it's the questions it awakens inside us, especially when we're used to solving problems, leading with clarity, or fixing what's broken.

But what do you do when you've prayed… and nothing moves? What do you do when the voice of God feels muted and your spiritual momentum stalls?

For many men, this becomes a pressure point. We begin to wonder:

- Did I miss something?
- Did I do something wrong?
- Why does God feel distant when I'm trying to stay faithful?

If you've ever walked through a season like this, you're not alone. What felt like spiritual silence at first became a deeper invitation into trust. God's silence is not absence—it's often the soil where deeper roots are formed. Sometimes silence is the wilderness where God shapes men—not with noise, but with His quiet, steady presence. The kind that doesn't shout but stays close. God's silence does not indicate that there's something wrong with you—it's often a sign that God is deepening your roots, not just expanding your reach. We'll explore what it reveals, what it builds in us, and how it becomes a pathway—not a punishment—for deeper spiritual formation.

THE EXPERIENCE OF SILENCE

I remember one morning in late winter I had just dropped the kids off at school and returned home, hoping for a quiet moment before the rest of the day pulled me in different directions. I sat in the living room, looking through the glass sliding doors. Outside, the wind howled and the snow whipped in sharp, swirling patterns, rattling the windows and twisting across the yard like a storm caught in its own rhythm. It was one of those deep Winnipeg winter mornings, about -25°C.

But that morning, it wasn't just the storm outside, it was my soul that felt quiet. The world beyond the glass was chaos, yet inside, there was a heavy stillness. Not peace exactly, but the kind of quiet that comes when you're waiting to hear from God and the silence stretches longer than expected. In the weeks leading up to that day, I had applied for several jobs, but the doors remained closed. My wife and I had launched our family-activity company, *Keiki Krate*, but the early momentum felt slow. We believed in our vision—to help families create meaningful moments together—but the profit wasn't matching our efforts. And in the middle of all of that, I felt the pressure building: to provide, to be strong, to figure it out.

And God… He felt silent. Not absent. Not cruel. Just… quiet.

I sat there that morning watching the wind sculpt the snow like miniature sand dunes in the desert; it was quite interesting to see the formations. The snow was very crisp and sand-like. What looked like small swirling white hills made me think of something deeper: how seasons shift, how what's happening on the surface doesn't always reflect what's forming beneath it. It was in that stillness that I sensed something subtle from God—not a booming word, but a gentle awareness: *Even this season is shaping you.* I didn't feel strong. I didn't feel like a spiritual leader or an inspired father or a man with clarity. I just felt…tired, and still. In the quiet, I knew God wasn't gone. He was teaching me how to walk by faith, not by feelings, and how to stay rooted when there's no emotional high—how to keep showing up in the silence.

But there was more stirring beneath the surface that day. Beneath the tiredness and the silence was a deeper ache— questions about whether I had chosen the harder path for my family in uprooting from Hawaii. I'm an island boy at heart—I miss the palm trees, the sand between my toes, the sound of the ocean—so, it wasn't the first time I found myself questioning the decision to move to Winnipeg. But the quiet cost of obedience was catching up with me in ways I hadn't expected: rebuilding friendships, reconstructing what "normal" looked like, letting go of rhythms that once defined who I was. There were days when I felt more lost than led, filled with more questions than answers.

My wife and I had felt peace that this was where the Lord was leading us. I knew Winnipeg would be cold and unfamiliar, but I hadn't wanted to stay in Hawaii, simply because it was more comfortable. We have a phrase we often say—a kind of family motto we've built our lives around: "Staying in love while raising kids and going where Jesus sends us." It sounds simple, but it carries weight when you're walking it out in real life. It's easy to say—but costly to live.

On that morning, I kept coming back to this belief, and I still do: the best place to be is always where God wants you to be—even if it's minus twenty-five.

Maybe I'll never know all the reasons why this is part of our story. Maybe it's not about my comfort—but about what my children, or even my grandchildren, will one day inherit from the seeds planted in this cold season. My desire is simply to keep trusting—and keep following His lead, wherever it takes us. I remember Kris Vallotton (from Bethel church in Redding, California) at an event in Kona, Hawaii, once said, "sometimes you're in a place and it has nothing to do with you, but everything to do with the people God wants you to impact".

On that icy morning in Winnipeg, I didn't even know how to pray. So, I just whispered something along these lines, "God, I don't need answers—I just need to know You're still with me." And maybe that's all He was waiting for—a heart still reaching upward in the quiet.

If you're in that kind of season right now—quiet, uncertain, in-between—know this: God is still shaping you, even in the silence.

I've grown since that cold winter morning, but the feeling still echoes from time to time when my soul aches for the warmth and ease of our island life. But it's part of the journey, trusting even when I can't trace what God is doing.

⸞⸞⸞

. . . .

God is still shaping you, even in the silence.

. . . .

I didn't know it then, but that quiet season was doing more in me than any answered prayer could have. Even Elijah—the bold prophet who called down fire—was shaped most deeply not in his public victory on Mount Carmel, but in the quiet of a cave where he confronted his fear, exhaustion, and need for God's whisper. It wasn't the dramatic moment that refined him, it was the stillness that followed, where he discovered God wasn't in the fire, the wind or the earthquake, but in the still gentle whisper that met him in his weakness.

WHAT SILENCE TEACHES: FORMATION IN THE QUIET

Silence may feel like the absence of activity, but it's often the furnace of spiritual formation. It's where unseen work happens—where God refines motives, exposes attachments, deepens trust, and forms unshakable character.

It doesn't mean doing nothing. It means resisting the urge to react, perform, or numb the discomfort. It's not zoning out, scrolling endlessly, or binging distractions to cope. It's being fully present with God, even when He seems quiet. It's sitting with your questions instead of escaping them. It's letting His Word read you. It's praying honest prayers, even if they're wordless. Stillness is a kind of internal surrender where striving ceases and listening begins.

Most of the transformation in a man's life doesn't happen in the loud visible moments of breakthrough—it happens in the quiet hidden places. This is where our faith is stretched, our pride is surrendered, and our inner life is recalibrated.

When God seems silent, He's often inviting us to:

- Develop roots, not just reach for fruit.
- Lean into trust, not just seek direction.
- Practice stillness by making space to hear God, versus chasing results.
- God's silence trains our spiritual ears to listen beyond the noise of demands, distractions, and internal pressure. Without the usual cues of clarity or confirmation, we start to realize how often we equate God's voice with external move-ment. Silence makes space for dependency—not performance. When God feels silent, when clear instructions aren't coming, we often default to routines, results, or reactions to regain a sense of

control. But it's exactly in that silence that God confronts this impulse. He reminds us that He is not asking us to perform; He's asking us to trust. Psalm 62:1 says, "Truly my soul finds rest in God: my salvation comes from him." That's not just poetic; it's practical. Rest is an act of trust. And trust is often clearest when you're surrounded by uncertainty.

Silence has a way of revealing our reflex to performance. We reach for results, rely on old strategies, or try to earn peace through effort. But silence invites us to stop striving and remember that God's presence isn't earned. It's received. And it forges a kind of strength that's not loud, but lasting.

You may not see what's happening in you while you wait—but something is forming beneath the surface. It's the hidden classroom where identity is forged not by what you do, but by who you become in the quiet. God isn't just preparing things for you—He's preparing you for the things to come. You're not being held back in this season—you're being held together. Sometimes God slows your pace so He can anchor your soul. It's not punishment, it's preservation. You may not be charging ahead, but you're not unraveling either. You're being sustained, refined, and quietly rebuilt from the inside out. In the silence, God isn't delaying your future; He's stabilizing your foundation.

This is the kind of formation that builds endurance, because endurance isn't built on hype or visibility, it's forged when you choose to keep showing up with no audience, no timeline, and no guaranteed outcome. In the silence, your motives are tested. Your heart is stretched. Your trust is deepened. That's where spiritual strength is born, not in the spotlight, but in the shadows where no one sees but God.

If you've ever wondered whether God does anything in the quiet, you're not alone. Some of the most powerful transformations in Scripture happened far away from the noise—hidden, slow, but deeply sacred. God is forming you, not forgetting you. The silence may feel like delay, but in God's hands—it's preparation. What's forming in the quiet today is what will anchor your legacy tomorrow.

ANCHORED IN THE QUIET: STORIES THAT SHOW THE WAY

Throughout Scripture, some of the deepest soul work happens not in the crowd or on the battlefield—but in the silence. God has always used quiet seasons to form leaders, refine purpose, and deepen identity. We're told that progress must be loud, visible, and fast. But formation doesn't work that way. It's slow. Hidden. Intentional. As Wharton professor and best-selling author of *Give and Think Again*, Adam Grant, wrote, "The most meaningful work often happens when no one is watching."[6]

I mentioned Elijah earlier. After calling down fire from heaven and confronting the prophets of Baal, Elijah finds himself drained, fearful, and alone. He retreats into the wilderness, exhausted and uncertain. But it's in the cave—not

---

[6] Give and Take, 2013, Penguin Books – Grant, A. (2013). *Give and take: Why helping others drives our success.* New York, NY: Penguin Books.

the mountaintop—where God meets him in a whisper. Not in fire, not in wind, not in earthquake—but in stillness (1 Kings 19:11–12).

Elijah didn't need more adrenaline—he needed realignment. When God asked, "What are you doing here?" (verse 13), it wasn't condemnation—it was clarity. It was the kind of clarity that cuts through the noise, not with new information, but with divine perspective. God wasn't just asking a question; He was helping Elijah see where fear had clouded his vision. The whisper reminded him that God hadn't changed, and neither had the calling. It wasn't a booming command but it was God's way of reminding Elijah that His presence isn't always loud, but it's always faithful. Elijah wasn't alone. He hadn't been disqualified. God met him in the quiet to recenter his heart and recommission his mission.

Elijah walked into the cave burned out and asking to die. But he walked out with renewed clarity and a redefined mission. He was no longer focused on his feelings of failure but anchored in the reality that God still had purpose for him. He was grounded in God's faithfulness, aware that the journey wasn't over, and rooted in the truth that calling doesn't disappear in difficult seasons—it often deepens.

Elijah isn't the only one. Joseph is a powerful example, not just of hardship, but of holy silence. After receiving a dream from God, he entered years of obscurity where everything around him seemed to contradict the promise. There were no reminders, no visions, no prophetic confirmations. Just betrayal from his brothers, false accusation, and long seasons of being forgotten. But in that time, even in prison, without any updates from heaven, he stewarded what was in his hands. He served. He waited. He interpreted dreams for others. And he kept showing up faithfully, even when he had every reason to give up.

When I moved to Winnipeg, I had to hold on to the last thing God said, because nothing in my present seemed to affirm it. Like Joseph, I had to keep trusting that God was still at work behind the scenes. Sometimes the silence isn't about punishment, but preparation. And when Joseph finally stood before Pharaoh, he wasn't just fulfilling a dream—he was stepping into a purpose that had been forged in faithfulness. (See Genesis 39 – 41.)

So, if you're still in the in-between, the cave, the prison, or the long pause between what God said and what you're seeing, don't assume nothing is happening. You're not stuck. You're being shaped. And when the time comes to step into what's next, you won't just be moving forward, you'll be moving forward formed, carrying wisdom, resilience, and a deeper dependence on God than when you began. Sometimes what God builds in you privately becomes the very strength others lean on publicly.

So, what do you do in the silence? You anchor yourself to what God has already said. You feed your soul with His truth. You stay connected to brothers who remind you who you are. You worship before you feel the breakthrough. You pray through the fog, not because you always feel Him, but because you trust He's still present.

What God builds in you privately can become the strength others lean on publicly.

I'm also in a season where God is deepening this in me again. I haven't graduated from the quiet. I'm still learning to listen, not with my ears only but with my posture. For me, that means slowing down enough to notice what's stirring beneath the surface. Sometimes it means journaling through my questions. Other times, it's bringing those questions into conversation with a brother I trust, because learning to listen to God often starts when you let someone else help carry what you can't yet make sense of alone.

So, if you feel like you're in the trenches, know that I'm right there beside you. This isn't a chapter I've just studied--it's one I'm still living. And together, we're learning to let God form the kind of strength that doesn't need a stage—it just needs surrender. As we'll explore in the next chapter, silence doesn't have to isolate you. It can initiate brotherhood. Sometimes the clearest direction comes not in louder answers, but in shared presence, where the weight is lighter simply because you're not carrying it alone.

LIVING IT OUT: PRAYING THROUGH THE SILENCE

Seasons of silence aren't empty, they're often where the deepest formation happens. Here are three ways to walk through them with intention and spiritual depth:

▶ **Where Am I Being Invited To Let Go?**
Take ten minutes this week to reflect or journal: What expectations, outcomes, or internal pressure am I carrying into this season? What might God be inviting me to release so I can receive instead of striving?

▶ **Who Am I Inviting Into The Quiet With Me?**
You weren't meant to walk through silence alone. This week, share with one trusted friend what God might be forming in you, even if it's still unclear.

▶ **What Truth Am I Holding Onto Right Now?**
Pick one scripture to anchor your soul this week, especially when God feels silent:

- **Psalm 46:10** "He says, 'Be still, and know that I am God; I will be exalted among the nations, I will be exalted in the earth.'"

- **Lamentations 3:26** "It is good to wait quietly for the salvation of the Lord."

- **Isaiah 30:15** "This is what the Sovereign Lord, the Holy One of Israel, says: 'In repentance and rest is your salvation, in quietness and trust is your strength, but you would have none of it.'"

chapter six

The Power of Brotherhood

I've come to realize that brotherhood is forged in fire—but it's sustained through intentionality.

The fire looks different for every man. Sometimes it's the pressure of provision. Sometimes it's the crushing weight of silence, loneliness, or leadership. In earlier chapters, we looked at those very moments, when God seems quiet, when purpose feels distant, when the climb feels steep. That is the fire. For me, this season looked like leaving behind the familiar, stepping into uncertainty, and navigating spiritual dryness that I didn't fully have the language to communicate. It meant confronting old wounds I thought I'd already dealt with, and learning to pray through silence, not just around it.

Brotherhood is forged in fire—but it's sustained through intentionality.

But while the fire may form something in us, it can't sustain us. That's where brotherhood comes in. Brotherhood is forged in shared experiences, in being seen without performing, and in standing shoulder-to-shoulder when life gets heavy. But what keeps it alive is not crisis; it's consistency. Brotherhood that lasts doesn't just show up in the fire, but it lingers long after, walking with you when the flames die down.

Brotherhood doesn't mean a man avoids every struggle. But it means he doesn't walk through it unseen. A true brother doesn't just catch you when you fall, he walks close enough to help you stay upright when the pressure mounts. Sometimes his presence is the reminder that you're not alone in the fight, and that makes all the difference.

For many men, especially those with distant or passive fathers, the idea of brotherhood is shaped not by depth but by duty—or by silence. The values you need to grow as a man might not always be modeled clearly. Even with siblings, you may not share clarity, conviction, or emotional presence; this has been my experience at least, and that of other men I've spoken to. I find that brotherhood is often built with those who walk in the same direction, not just those who share the same DNA.

One of the men God has used to sharpen me in this season is my friend Jacob. We check in weekly, sometimes it's a full conversation, sometimes it's a prayer, sometimes it's just a simple question that cuts through the fog and reminds me what matters. He doesn't just pat me on the back and say, "Keep going." He fights beside me. He holds the bigger picture when I lose sight of it. He's the kind of man you want in the trenches—not just because he'll pray with you, but because he'll remind you who you are when you forget. He's what I imagine David's mighty men were like, not perfect, but present. Not just warriors in battle, but loyal friends in exile. In a world that often trains men to isolate, bottle it up, and carry their burdens alone, brothers like Jacob are rare, and essential.

But it's not just about what brotherhood has done for me. It's also about what I've learned to offer others. Years ago, I met Zach in Hawaii. A couple of years later, we reconnected unexpectedly in New York while he was walking through a difficult season. Something in me knew I couldn't just catch up—I needed to walk with him, pray with him, speak life over him. I didn't think much of it at the time—it felt like the natural thing to do. But years later, Zach still reminds me how much that season marked him. How the simple act of showing up, checking in, and calling out purpose helped him find his footing again. That's what brotherhood does. It doesn't fix everything, but it stays present. It doesn't walk away when things get hard. Sometimes, just knowing someone still sees you is enough to keep going.

In 2012, during one of the hardest transitions of my life, I moved to Hawaii. I was a bachelor then, navigating a recent breakup, sorting through deep questions, and recognizing that parts of my life needed pruning, healing, and growth. That's when I met Jim, an older man who became a lifelong mentor and friend.

At that time, I was used to leaders who led from position, holding authority tightly, protecting their image, and rarely letting anyone see behind the curtain. Vulnerability wasn't part of the model. Strength was measured by how polished or in control you appeared. But Jim was different.

We made time to meet up regularly. I'd bring my questions about growth, leadership, and calling, and he'd ask thoughtful, sometimes challenging questions in return. He didn't offer quick fixes. He challenged me, gently, but clearly. He shared parts of his own journey, not to impress, but to invite. There was a steady humility in him that gave me permission to be real. He didn't try to lead by domination or distance, but by proximity and presence. He would listen carefully, offer insights from his own life, and always ask, "What's God been stirring in you lately?" That kind of leadership shaped me deeply.

Jim showed me what brotherhood could become, not just side-by-side friendships, but intentional, sharpening relationships that shape how you lead, heal, and show up for others. He modeled what it means to be fully present by making space in his schedule to connect, to be spiritually anchored by consistently pointing me back to God's truth, and emotionally available by listening with empathy, asking honest questions, and offering his own story with vulnerability.

That's why I believe so strongly in brotherhood. I've seen what happens when men show up with courage, humility, and consistency, for each other.

WHY SO MANY MEN MISS IT

If brotherhood is so vital, why do so many men struggle to experience it? The truth is most of us were never shown how. Brotherhood isn't something many of us saw modeled well. In a lot of homes, emotional distance was normalized. We were taught how to compete, how to protect, how to be strong, but rarely how to be honest about what was really going on inside. Not honest in the sense of telling the truth about a situation, but honest about fear, grief, insecurity, temptation. Honest about weakness. Vulnerability wasn't encouraged—it may have been shamed.

Brotherhood is different from other familial bonds. It's not just about shared DNA or even shared history. It's a sacred commitment to walk alongside someone with intentionality, accountability, and love. It's about knowing and being known, not just being around each other. And when no one teaches you how to do that, you either mimic dysfunction or isolate in silence.

In a perfect world, fathers and spiritual mentors would model this. But in reality, many men are discipled by absence or performance, not presence and emotional courage. We don't need more male influencers; we need more men who influence through presence.

→ **What silent rules did you absorb about being a man—and how have they shaped your ability to let others in?**

As psychologist Warren Farrell and John Gray point out in The Boy Crisis, when boys grow up without strong, emotionally engaged male role models, they often struggle with emotional regulation, purpose, and relational connection.

The absence of consistent father figures or intentional male mentorship leaves a gap in emotional literacy and identity formation.[7]

This lack of mentorship is compounded by a cultural narrative that celebrates self-sufficiency over connection. From Batman to Jason Bourne, we're handed this image of the lone hero—the man who fights alone, figures it all out, and never asks for help. But that picture has left a generation of men emotionally starved. We've learned to admire isolation, but not intimacy. And in real life, that kind of disconnection doesn't build strength, it breeds burnout. It's not just an emotional issue—it's a health issue.

One landmark study from Brigham Young University found that chronic loneliness is as dangerous as smoking fifteen cigarettes a day.[8] Isolation rewires our nervous systems, lowers resilience, and increases the risk of depression and anxiety.

And spiritually? The consequences run even deeper, because when a man walks alone, he becomes more susceptible to temptation, burnout, and despair. Sometimes it's pride. Sometimes it's shame. Sometimes it's just fear of being exposed. But whatever the reason, isolation becomes the silent killer.

---

[7] The Boy Crisis – Farrell, W., & Gray, J. (2018). *The boy crisis: Why our boys are struggling and what we can do about it.* Dallas, TX: BenBella Books.
[8] Holt-Lunstad, J., Smith, T. B., Baker, M., Harris, T., & Stephenson, D. (2015). Loneliness and social isolation as risk factors for mortality: A meta-analytic review. *Perspectives on Psychological Science, 10*(2), 227–237. https://doi.org/10.1177/1745691614568352

→ **The enemy doesn't need to destroy a man publicly if he can keep him disconnected privately.**

Organizational psychologist Adam Grant has consistently emphasized that leaders who cultivate trusted peer relationships, and stay connected to circles of accountability, outperform those who operate in isolation.[9] These peer bonds are grounded in mutual trust, where each person feels safe enough to be challenged and supported. Real trust is when you can be honest without fear—and still be sharpened.

Growth doesn't happen just because you're in community. It happens in the kind of community where honesty is safe, accountability is welcomed, and spiritual truth is spoken in love. In performance-driven or fear-based environments, growth can be stunted, or completely shut down. But in healthy brotherhood, where vulnerability is met with grace and truth, growth multiplies.

I've sat across from men—leaders, husbands, dads—who confessed they had no one to talk to about their hidden battles. One man once said to me, "I feel like I'm dying in the spotlight. Everyone sees me, but no one knows me." That sentence really had me thinking, because I've felt it too. It's the ache of being visible but not vulnerable. Of being celebrated for your gifting, while quietly crumbling under the weight of expectations. In those moments, what we need most isn't more applause—it's connection. Not just someone to cheer us on, but someone who knows the cost of our climb.

---

[9] Grant, A. (2014). *Give and take: Why helping others drives our success.* New York, NY: Penguin Books.

> **Healthy brotherhood, where vulnerability is met with grace and truth, growth multiplies.**

WHAT DOES TRUE BROTHERHOOD LOOK LIKE?

The question isn't, "Do you have friends?" It's, "Do you have men who know what's really going on—and still choose to walk with you?"

→ **Who know the real you—the stuff you don't post or polish?**
→ **Who challenge you to rise—not just to vent?**
→ **Who remind you of your calling when you're tempted to forget it?**

As Dietrich Bonhoeffer said in *Life Together*, "The person who loves their dream of community will destroy community, but the person who loves those around them will create community."[10] Brotherhood isn't a dream. It's a decision. A slow, costly, beautiful decision to walk with others in truth. This is the kind of brother who listens when you're low and doesn't flinch when you get real. He's not just a friend for fun, but a man who holds space for your truth, who challenges you, intercedes for you, and reminds you of who you are when you've forgotten. He's consistent, not perfect.

---

[10] Bonhoeffer, D. (1954). *Life together: The classic exploration of Christian community.* (J. W. Doberstein, Trans.). New York, NY: Harper & Row.

Present, not performative. He's a brother who doesn't rescue you from the pain but walks with you through it.

Brotherhood doesn't happen by accident. It's forged by choice, vulnerability, and shared commitment. If you're reading this and realizing you don't have that kind of brother, you're not alone. And it's not too late. The first step is never grand—it's honest. The good news? Brotherhood isn't found; it's built. And you can start building it now.

HOW BROTHERHOOD IS BUILT, NOT FOUND

Brotherhood isn't something you stumble into—it's something you fight for. Too many men sit around waiting for the perfect group, the perfect friend, or the perfect church to hand them connection on a silver platter. But brotherhood doesn't come that way. It isn't delivered—it's developed.

Jesus didn't wait for us to reach out—He moved toward us first. Brotherhood begins the same way. Someone has to go first, and as men of faith, that someone is often us. Real connection starts when you're willing to go first: to ask the deeper question, and to say the first honest sentence. I've seen this happen firsthand. A guy I was walking with once opened up during a group meet-up—not with a sermon or a speech, but with a simple line: "I'm not doing okay, and I don't want to fake it anymore." That one moment shifted the whole room. It gave other men permission to take off the mask. And from that moment forward, something unspoken began to form—a circle of trust that couldn't be manufactured, only revealed.

Building brotherhood requires intentionality. And often, interruption. It grows slowly, through shared struggle, honest conversations, and repeated presence. It's less about finding the right people and more about becoming the kind of man others can trust with their truth.

> → **What if you stopped waiting for brotherhood and started building it—one text, one question, one prayer at a time?**

Jon Tyson, in his book *The Intentional Father*, talks about creating intentional rhythms of male connection and discipleship. He says, "You can't microwave masculinity—it must be slow-cooked in the presence of other men."[11]

That's the invitation: not to rush into shallow groups, but to build brotherhood through consistent presence, check-ins, shared habits, and through bringing your real self to the table, over and over again.

Brotherhood is built through:

- **Presence over performance**—showing up when it's inconvenient.
- **Consistency over charisma**—choosing relationship even when the spark fades.
- **Courage over comfort**—saying what's real, even when it's vulnerable.

---

[11] Tyson, J. (2021). The intentional father: A practical guide to raise sons of courage and character. Grand Rapids, MI: Baker Books.

Who do you need to reach out to this week—not because it's easy, but because it's essential?

James Clear, in his work on habit formation, says, "Every action you take is a vote for the type of person you want to become."[12] Brotherhood works the same way. Every honest conversation. Every intentional follow-up. Every time you pray together or listen instead of fixing—that's a vote for the kind of man, and the kind of community, you're building.

Proverbs 18:24 reminds us, "…there is a friend who sticks closer than a brother." That's not just poetry—it's a picture of what's possible when men choose loyalty, vulnerability, and commitment over isolation.

Even Dr. Martin Luther King Jr., who carried a national burden, never walked alone. He shared prayer, counsel, and long nights with Ralph Abernathy, his closest brother in the fight for justice.[13] That brotherhood was forged in fire, but it helped fuel a movement.

That said, there are subtle pitfalls that can slowly erode even well-intentioned connections:

- Trying to impress instead of invest.
- Letting momentum fade after a few honest conversations.

---

[12] Clear, J. (2018). Atomic habits: An easy & proven way to build good habits & break bad ones. New York, NY: Avery.

[13] Abernathy, R. (1989). *And the walls came tumbling down: An autobiography*. New York, NY: Harper & Row.

- Brotherhood isn't maintained by emotion—it's maintained by intention. And here's the truth: you don't have to be perfect to build it. You just have to be present.

The greatest brotherhoods don't come from shared interests—they come from shared surrender. At some point, brotherhood stops being about what you need—and starts becoming about who you're willing to stand with.

BECOMING A BROTHER WHO FIGHTS FOR OTHERS

The most powerful brotherhoods are forged not in shared convenience, but in shared commitment. At some point, every man must decide whether he will simply seek support, or become the kind of brother others can lean on.

Brotherhood isn't just about being known. It's about showing up when it's costly. It's about carrying one another's burdens when it would be easier to walk away. Galatians 6:2 puts it plainly: "Carry each other's burdens, and in this way you will fulfill the law of Christ."

This kind of brotherhood isn't reactive—it's proactive. It says:

- I'll check in, even if you don't reach out.
- I'll speak truth when you're drifting.
- I'll stand with you when others fall away.

→ **Who's carrying something heavy right now that God may be asking you to help lift?**

One of the most Christlike things you can do is fight for your brother's freedom, healing, or clarity when he's lost sight of it himself.

A few years ago, a friend of mine was walking through deep disappointment—family conflict, the passing of his dad, financial pressure, and a deep sense of spiritual apathy. He wasn't asking for help, but the Holy Spirit kept nudging me. So, I showed up. Texted. Prayed. Called. Invited. We talked for hours more than once. Months later, he told me, "You reminded me I wasn't too far gone. I didn't believe in me—but you still did."

That's the mark of real brotherhood. Not the absence of struggle—but the presence of someone who refuses to let you sink without a fight.

When men begin to walk this way, something powerful happens: isolation shatters, cycles break. Healing doesn't stay contained, it spreads. As one man finds freedom, he often becomes a vessel for someone else's breakthrough. Emotional wounds begin to mend. Past shame loses its grip. Generational patterns start to shift.

Brotherhood isn't about rescuing. It's about reflecting Christ: standing in the gap, bearing burdens, celebrating progress. And sometimes, just staying through the silence.

Real brotherhood is the presence of someone who refuses to let you sink without a fight.

John Eldredge in *Wild At Heart*, puts it like this: "A man must have a mission—something to fight for, and someone to fight with."[14] Brotherhood gives us both. It reminds us that the mission is never just about *you*. It's about what God wants to build through *us*.

> → **What would happen if every man reading this chapter committed to fight for just one other man this year?**

Brotherhood isn't just a place to be known, it's a place to be shaped. A forge. A fire. A mirror that helps you see yourself more clearly and a shoulder that reminds you you're not carrying your burdens alone. But even the strongest brotherhoods can falter when we confuse being connected with being conformed.

You weren't made to become a copy of the men around you. Brotherhood was never meant to blur the uniqueness of your journey; it was meant to give you the courage to walk it. If we're not careful, the very circle meant to sharpen us can become the place we begin to compare ourselves. Who's

---

[14] Eldredge, J. (2001). *Wild at heart: Discovering the secret of a man's soul.* Nashville, TN: Thomas Nelson.

growing faster? Who seems more whole? Who's ahead? But real brotherhood doesn't feed competition. It fights it. It says, "You don't have to be like me. You just have to be you, and I'll walk with you as you become more of that."

That's the invitation as we turn the page: to keep showing up, not just for others, but for your own God-given journey—to stop measuring your life by someone else's map, to walk in step with Jesus—even if your pace looks different.

The next step isn't comparison. It's courage. Your journey is holy, even if it's hidden. Let's talk about that next.

LIVING IT OUT: BUILDING BROTHERHOOD IN REAL LIFE

Brotherhood isn't built by accident—it's built through small steps of presence, honesty, and courage.

▶ **Where Am I Being Invited To Show Up For Someone?**

Take ten minutes this week to reflect:
- Who's one brother I've lost touch with or feel prompted to reach out to?
- What small step of presence can I offer, without needing it to be perfect?

▶ **Who Am I Letting In Right Now?**

You weren't meant to walk alone.
- Share something real with one trusted brother this week.
- Ask a question that opens space for honesty: "How's your heart, really?"

▶ **What Truth Am I Holding Onto In Brotherhood?**

Choose one scripture to carry this week:
- **Proverbs 17:17** "A friend loves at all times, and a brother is born for a time of adversity."
- **Proverbs 27:17** "As iron sharpens iron, so one person sharpens another."
- **Galatians 6:2** "Carry each other's burdens, and in this way you will fulfill the law of Christ."

chapter seven

Embracing Your Unique Journey

Not every man's journey looks the same—and that's the point. In a world that shouts for uniformity and rewards comparison, God's work in your life may appear slower, quieter, or completely different than what you expected. That doesn't make it less holy. It makes it yours.

Comparison is one of the quickest ways to suffocate your sense of calling. We see another man's success, his speed, or his spotlight—and we begin to doubt the value of our own story. But God isn't forming clones. He's shaping sons. I see it in my own boys. Same parents, same home, but completely different wiring. One is all energy and questions, the other moves slower, more thoughtfully. They don't grow at the same pace, and I don't expect them to. My job as their father isn't to mold them into the same person, but to guide them each according to who they're becoming. Isn't that how God walks with us too? And He doesn't rush the process.

Comparison quickly suffocates your sense of calling.

Think of Joseph: his path to leadership was marked by betrayal, slavery, and prison. It didn't look like favor—but it was. Joseph was betrayed, sold, falsely accused, and imprisoned. From the outside, it looked like failure. But through every setback, God was positioning him, building integrity, discernment, and the kind of character that could carry influence without being crushed by it. The favor wasn't just in the outcome; it was in the formation. Sometimes God's favor looks like closed doors that keep us on the path He designed.

Joseph waited over a decade for his dream to come to pass. Moses spent forty years in obscurity before leading Israel: he didn't step into his assignment until age eighty. God isn't slow—He's strategic.

Both had seasons where it seemed like God was taking too long, but in hindsight, we see He was preparing them to carry what was coming. As a dad, I'm learning this too. Sometimes my kids want something now, but as their father, I know the right thing at the wrong time can do more harm than good. Waiting doesn't mean God has forgotten; it means He's preparing.

Still, many of us live with the weight of invisible timelines. Maybe you thought you'd be further along by now. Maybe your life doesn't look like the men you follow or admire. Maybe you've been faithful, but unseen. Obedient, but overlooked. And quietly, you've started wondering, *Did I miss it? Did I mess it up? Is something wrong with me?*

That's why embracing your unique journey is one of the most freeing, and faith-filled decisions you'll ever make. It's the point where you stop measuring your progress by someone else's map—and begin trusting the path God has for you.

→ **What expectations—spoken or unspoken—have shaped how you see your life's pace or value?**
→ **Have you ever felt behind, even though you were walking in obedience?**

Let's be honest: part of what makes this difficult is the pressure we carry from how we were raised. For many of us, that pressure starts with the father wound—not just the pain of what was done, but the confusion of what was never said. We're not spending this whole chapter digging into the father wound—but we'd be missing something if we didn't acknowledge how early voices shape our internal compass. Because sometimes the loudest critics we battle aren't out there—they're inside us. And they sound an awful lot like people we were once desperate to please.

The loudest critics can sound a lot like people we were once desperate to please.

THE PAIN OF COMPARISON IN FAMILY

Growing up, I don't remember a lot of conversation about what made each of us unique. There weren't outright comparisons, but I do remember moments where one sibling's success was celebrated, and the others weren't acknowledged. It left questions lingering: *Am I enough? Am I doing it right?* Sometimes, the loudest beliefs are born from what no one ever said out loud.

I'll never forget a moment years after our childhood when my younger brother quietly said, "I feel like the black sheep of the family." It caught me off guard. No one had ever labeled him that. We grew up in the same home, attended the same private school, had access to the same privileges my older siblings hadn't. And yet—he felt unseen. That stayed with me. It made me start listening differently. I began to pay closer attention to how he interpreted things, and to the subtle dynamics between him and my parents. Where was that seed planted? And how could it be reversed?

Parenting is complex. Sometimes, without realizing it, a mom or dad may naturally connect more easily with one child over another, maybe because their personalities or love languages line up, and without ever meaning to, it sends a signal to the other child that they don't quite measure up. We don't always see it in the moment. And no matter how intentional we try to be as parents, we'll never get it all right. That's why we need God's help to shepherd not just our children's behavior, but their hearts.

RUN YOUR OWN RACE

By now, you've done the deep work—facing silence, wrestling through internal battles, and learning to walk with brothers. Now God's inviting you to trust the shape of your own story.

You weren't made to mimic someone else's calling. You were made to embody Christ's call in the form He's shaping in *you*.

> → **Success isn't about matching someone else's pace—it's about walking faithfully in your own assignment.**

When you realize your journey is meant to be different, and that it's actually part of God's design—not a detour—you begin to walk lighter. Freer. More present. You don't have to prove anything. You don't have to run someone else's race. You just have to keep saying yes to the path God has for *you*.

You may remember how I shared earlier about our transition from Hawaii to Canada. What I didn't talk about then was the quiet storm of comparison that hit me once we started settling in—the kind that doesn't announce itself, but slowly erodes your sense of purpose. I knew the shift would be significant. But I didn't expect how deeply the silence and invisibility would settle in once the bags were unpacked. The people were somewhat kind—but the cold air, unfamiliar customs, and quiet isolation made the transition jarring. There were no palm trees. No oceans. Just a slow unraveling of everything familiar.

I had spent years investing in community development, discipling men, and helping to shape community alongside other leaders. And then suddenly, I was in a place where no one knew my name or my history. There were days I questioned everything, my value, my timing, even my obedience.

But beneath the surface, what I was really wrestling with was comparison.

At close to hitting forty, I imagined I'd be further ahead—leading a movement, traveling the world, making an impact. Instead, I was packing groceries, shoveling snow, filling out immigration paperwork, and trying to keep my family afloat in a country that didn't feel like home yet. Meanwhile, friends in other parts of the world were buying homes, starting businesses, and posting highlight reels of wins I couldn't fully relate to.

Comparison didn't just steal my joy; it was challenging my identity. I began to question whether my slow season meant I was failing—whether God had skipped me or obedience had backfired.

→ **Have you ever obeyed God and still felt like you were falling behind?**

But here's what I learned: comparison rarely accounts for context. It just flashes outcomes. And when your season looks hidden, the temptation is to assume God is absent, when in fact, He may be doing His deepest work underground.

I had to confront the pride I didn't realize I was carrying, the idea that obedience should equal immediate reward, and the belief that if I was really faithful, I'd have the results to show for it. But faithfulness doesn't always look like fruit right away. Sometimes it looks like grit. Like showing up when no one sees. Like working a job you're overqualified for while trusting that God sees every unseen seed.

I'll be honest: there were days I felt disappointed. Not quite depressed but weighed down by a mix of discouragement and quiet frustration. I'd get messages from friends doing big things, speaking at conferences, buying their second properties, getting big promotions at work. Meanwhile, I was measuring flour at the bakery and wondering if God had misplaced me.

Comparison has a way of shrinking your view until all you can see is what you lack. And God had to pull me out of that pit, not by changing my circumstances right away, but by realigning my perspective. I realize I wasn't stuck but instead, I was being shaped.

Hidden seasons aren't wasted, they're where roots go deep. Ecclesiastes 3:1 says, "There is a time for everything, and a season for every activity under the heavens." The Amplified Bible says, "a time appointed."

That line, "a time appointed", wrecks me in the best way. Because, if God appoints seasons, then slowness isn't failure; it's formation. And if there's a season for everything, then trying to harvest in the planting season will only lead to frustration. I had been trying to force fruit when God was still shaping my roots. Think about it: What happens if you try to harvest too early? The fruit is underdeveloped. Bitter. Fragile. That's what happens to us when we try to live out of sync with God's timing. We step into stages we're not prepared for. We place pressure on outcomes instead of partnering with the process.

**Comparison distorts your vision until all
you notice is lack.**

When we live out of God's timing, we move in panic, not peace. We push for platforms we're not ready to carry. We mistake delay for denial, and process for punishment. But God is not slow—He's strategic. He's not merely preparing the blessing for you; He's preparing you for the blessing. And sometimes the real test isn't whether you can build, it's whether you can be still. Whether you can stay planted when no one's watching. That's what I had to learn in that season. To walk my own path, at my own pace. With God's presence as my pacesetter.

Are you willing to trust God's pace, even when it doesn't match your expectations?

SHEDDING THE WEIGHT OF UNREALISTIC TIMELINES

Let's be honest, culture comes with a clock.

- By twenty-five: have a degree.
- By thirty: own a home.
- By thirty-five: be not just successful, but very successful in your career.
- By forty: lead something worth talking about.

And if you're not on schedule, the message is loud and clear: You're behind. But God doesn't work off culture's countdown. His timeline looks very different. **It starts with hidden obedience**—where you say yes without applause. **Then comes character shaping**—where your heart gets aligned before your name gets known. Promotion? It's sometimes delayed, not because you're forgotten, but because you're still being formed. And the goal? Not quick applause, but lasting impact.

In my own story, I had the passion. I had the plans. But God was building something deeper: resilience, endurance, maturity, the kind of strength that can carry weight without crumbling. And now, looking back, I see it clearly: The delay wasn't punishment. It was preparation.

God isn't limited by our clocks; He's anchored in legacy. When He calls Himself the God of Abraham, Isaac, and Jacob, He's not just making a poetic statement. He's revealing a truth: His plans stretch beyond a single lifespan.

David dreamed of building the temple, but Solomon fulfilled it. Why? Because sometimes your role is to lay the groundwork for someone else's breakthrough. And that's not failure—it's faithfulness.

We obsess over productivity because we fear our mortality. But God, who sees the end from the beginning, isn't panicked by your pace. He's forming something bigger than a personal brand. He's writing a generational story. He may not fulfill every dream in your lifetime, but He will be faithful to every purpose across your bloodline. So, if your timeline feels off, breathe. God's not late. He's just working with a bigger calendar than you can see.

> → **Where have you been measuring your life by someone else's clock?**

Freedom begins when we surrender the timeline and trust the Author. The real question isn't, "Am I late?" It's, "Am I becoming the man God is forming in this season?"

Some of the most important things God does in you won't be fast. But they'll be lasting.

As C.S. Lewis wrote in *Mere Christianity*, "You are never too old to become younger."[15] It's a reminder that renewal and growth have no age limit. A similar phrase, often attributed to Lewis, puts it this way: "You are never too old to set another goal or to dream a new dream". He didn't publish his first major work until his forties. Nelson Mandela didn't become president until after twenty-seven years in prison. Their timelines didn't disqualify them, they prepared them.

So, surround yourself with voices who remind you: God's timing is not a competition; it's calling. His pace, not the world's, is where peace is found. The real victory isn't in speed, it's in faithfulness.

Let God reset your pace. Let Him rewrite your calendar. Let Him remind you that you're not behind, you're becoming the man He created you to be.

---

[15] (Lewis, Mere Christianity 1952/2001,). – Lewis, C. S. (2001). *Mere Christianity*. New York, NY: HarperOne. (Original work published 1952).

———

Before purpose shows up in power, it often starts in silence. You may feel buried, but in the Kingdom, buried often means planted. Jesus said, "Very truly I tell you, unless a kernel of wheat falls to the ground and dies, it remains only a single seed. But if it dies, it produces many seeds" (John 12:24). Don't mistake the soil for a grave; it might just be the garden. That's what we're stepping into next.

**Don't mistake the soil for a grave;
it might just be the garden.**

The Climb Cycle

LIVING IT OUT: EMBRACING YOUR UNIQUE JOURNEY

Comparison distorts the view, but alignment restores your vision. Here'p9s how to walk forward with clarity, faith, and peace.

▶ **What Are You Walking Out Of?**
Take five quiet minutes and ask:
- Where am I still carrying someone else's timeline?
- What pressures or expectations are making me feel "behind"?
- What season does God have me in, and how can I honor it?

▶ **Who Are You Walking With?**
Reach out to one man you trust and ask:
- "How are you doing at trusting God's timing in this season?"
- Share your struggle honestly and listen without trying to fix. Walk together.

▶ **What Are You Walking Toward?**
Choose one of these scriptures and carry it with you this week:
- Ecclesiastes 3:1 "There is a time for everything, and a season for every activity under heaven."
- Psalm 37:23 "The Lord makes firm the steps of the one who delights in him."

- Isaiah 60:22 "The least of you will become a thousand, the smallest a mighty nation. I am the Lord; in its time I will do this swiftly."

chapter eight

The Seed of Purpose

Purpose doesn't always arrive as a lightning bolt. Sometimes, it's a seed—small, buried, and quiet. Before it grows, it disappears. Before it bears fruit, it breaks open. That's how the Kingdom of God works—and often, that's how purpose unfolds in a man's life.

Remember how I mentioned Joseph? When he was young, God gave him a dream of influence, leadership, and legacy. But what followed didn't look like purpose—it looked like abandonment. But underground, something deeper was taking root: trust, integrity, and dependence on God. These weren't just traits Joseph needed for survival; they were qualities that would one day shape a nation. God was forming a man who could handle power without being corrupted by it. Joseph's journey shows us a powerful truth: purpose is planted long before it's platformed.

Have you ever felt like the very thing God promised seems to be hiding beneath the surface? That's what seeds do. They disappear before they rise. And maybe that's where you are right now—still in the soil. Still waiting. Still wondering if what you carry actually matters.

Don't despise the hiddenness. Don't run from the slow. God is not in a rush with what He's building in you. As Jesus said, it is like a mustard seed, which is the smallest of all seeds on earth. Yet when planted, it grows and becomes the largest of all garden plants, with such big branches that the birds can perch in its shade" (Mark 4:31–32).

Small doesn't mean insignificant. Hidden doesn't mean forgotten. Delayed doesn't mean denied. What matters isn't how quickly you rise—it's how deeply you're rooted.

**What matters isn't how fast you rise,
but how deeply you're rooted.**

WHEN PURPOSE FEELS DORMANT

I didn't always feel like I was walking in purpose. There have been seasons—deep, silent, and slow—where everything in me asked God, "What is this all for?"

One of those seasons came when I took a job at a commercial bakery. At first, it sounded like a good opportunity—I figured I'd learn how to bake desserts, maybe even pick up a new skill. But it turned out to be far from the charming little shop I had imagined. This was large-scale industrial baking: massive ovens blasting at 375 degrees, and training shifts that started at 12 a.m., when your body and soul feel half asleep. Opening those furnace doors in the middle of the night felt like getting punched in the chest with heat.

The man assigned to train me didn't even know I was coming that first night. He was a year from retirement, tough as nails, and had the kind of mouth people politely call *colorful*. But under the cursing and gruffness, he was surprisingly open. We started talking about parenting and fatherhood. He told me he had got divorced after ten years of marriage (this was over three decades ago) and that, honestly, he had never wanted to be a dad. A passing relationship had turned permanent, and now he had sons he cared for deeply—but he regretted not being equipped for fatherhood. "I just didn't have the tools," he said.

Night after night, I worked those early hours beside him. And somewhere in the routine and exhaustion, I began to feel the nudge of the Holy Spirit—not to preach, but to pray. He took a lot of smoke breaks, and I could tell something heavy was resting on him. And I realized I wasn't there just to learn to bake. I was there to embody the presence of God in a place most people would overlook, to intercede for a man carrying decades of regret, and to serve, quietly, with spiritual awareness. Sometimes your assignment isn't about what you do, it's about who you're becoming in the process.

I started to think about Joseph: how God used him in the hidden places—in prison, in Potiphar's house—long before the palace. Joseph didn't need a platform to be faithful. He just needed to be present and attuned to what God was doing. That bakery wasn't glamorous, but it was sacred. It became part of my training ground for spiritual maturity, for quiet obedience, and for learning how to be faithful with small things when no one else is watching.

→ **Have you ever asked God, "Why am I here—doing *this*—when I thought I was made for more?"**

FAITHFUL STEWARDSHIP: WHEN SEEDS BECOME ASSIGNMENT

I believe there's a point in every man's life where the question shifts from "What is my purpose?" to "How am I stewarding what's already been planted?" It's not just about dreaming anymore—it's about cultivating, protecting, nurturing and showing up with consistency, even when results are slow.

Os Guinness, in his book *The Call* reminds us that "Calling is the truth that God calls us to Himself so decisively, that everything we are, everything we do, and everything we have is invested with a special devotion, dynamism, and direction."[16]

The word *devotion* stood out to me. It made me think of a farmer tending his soil. He doesn't rush the harvest or dig up the seed to check its progress. He waters. He watches. He waits. Because he knows the value of what's buried, even when no one else sees it. That's the kind of devotion calling requires. Not recognition. Not applause. Not a fast return, but a daily surrender; it is the quiet discipline of staying faithful to the work God gave you, even when it feels slow, small, or unseen.

Seeds don't just need water. They need a gardener, someone who watches over the soil, clears the weeds, enriches the

---

[16] Guinness, O. (2003). *The call: Finding and fulfilling the central purpose of your life* (Rev. ed.). Thomas Nelson.

ground, and protects the fragile sprout from harsh conditions. A good gardener knows the seed must break open before it ever breaks through. And he understands that growth isn't just about results; it's about what's happening beneath the surface.

In the same way, God calls us to tend what He's planted in us, not with striving, but with patience. Not with control, but with trust. Stewardship looks like showing up daily, doing the slow work of nurturing what no one else sees yet, and believing that something sacred is unfolding, even in the dark. That's what stewardship looks like: not obsessing over outcomes but remaining faithful with what's in your hand.

Maybe your assignment isn't glamorous right now. Maybe it doesn't look like anyone else's. But if God has planted it in your life, then He's also given you the grace to nurture it.

Let that be enough. Let that be holy.

BECOMING FRUITFUL IN THE RIGHT SEASON

Just like no farmer expects a harvest the day after planting, we can't expect our purpose to mature overnight. There's a process—a holy unfolding that takes time, trust, and tending. As Galatians 6:9 reminds us, "Let us not grow weary in doing good, for at the proper time we will reap a harvest if we do not give up." Purpose ripens in stages. It grows in silence. It's pruned through faithfulness.

One of the greatest dangers is rushing a season we were meant to receive slowly. Abraham was given a clear promise by God that he and Sarah would have a son. But when the waiting grew long and faith turned to frustration, he took matters into his own hands. At Sarah's suggestion, he slept with her servant Hagar and fathered Ishmael. Though God still blessed Ishmael, this decision brought heartache, division, and consequences that rippled through generations.

Purpose ripens in stages. It grows in silence. It's pruned through faithfulness.

It's a cautionary tale. One that reminds us, trying to force God's hand rarely leads to peace. Discernment matters. Timing matters. Purpose doesn't just require movement; it requires maturity.

So where are you right now? Not where do you want to be—but where has God placed you? Are you still in the soil? Still waiting? Still wondering? Hold steady. The seed hasn't been forgotten. And neither have you.

SUSTAINING PURPOSE AFTER PROMISE

Even when the seed finally breaks the surface and bears fruit, the work isn't over. Just ask David. After years of anointing without a crown, exile, betrayal, and wilderness refining, he finally stepped into kingship. But that didn't mean his fire stayed burning automatically. The Psalms give us a window into his inner life, moments where he pleaded with God to revive him, to restore joy, to search his heart. His greatest victories didn't remove his need for God; they deepened it. David understood that the same God who planted the seed was the One who had to keep it alive.

In Psalm 51, after one of his deepest moral failures, David prays, "Restore to me the joy of your salvation and grant me a willing spirit, to sustain me" (verse 12). That wasn't a prayer for position or protection, it was a prayer for renewal.

Purpose is not just about reaching a destination; it's about maintaining devotion once you get there. A tree still needs water long after it bears fruit. The same is true for you. Stewardship isn't just for the beginning—it's for the entire journey.

THE GROWTH CYCLE OF PURPOSE

Seed → Soil → Struggle → Sprout → Stewardship → Fruit

- **Seed**—The God-given idea or vision begins.
- **Soil**—Hiddenness, waiting, and formation in obscurity.
- **Struggle**—Resistance, setbacks, and refining seasons.
- **Sprout**—Early beginnings, glimpses of growth.
- **Stewardship**—Commitment to nurturing the small faithfully.
- **Fruit**—Tangible impact begins to emerge over time. Even fruit-bearing seasons include pruning—to protect the plant and redirect growth where it's needed most.

Discernment is key in each phase. We often want to skip steps or leap ahead, but spiritual growth doesn't work like that. Abraham was promised Isaac, but when he tried to take matters into his own hands and fathered Ishmael, it led to generations of unintended consequences. Don't shortcut your season. Learn to ask God not just what you're called to, but when and how. Each part of the process has a purpose.

You might feel like everyone else is sprouting while you're still in the soil, but comparison kills clarity. Trust your pace. Trust His timing. God is still growing something in you, even if no one else sees it yet.

As author James Clear writes in *Atomic Habits,* "Every action you take is a vote for the type of person you wish to become."[17] Purpose is rarely one grand leap; it's often the accumulation of small, faithful steps in the right direction. So stay rooted. Stay faithful. The fruit may not come fast, but it will come

Every seed carries weight—but not all at once. The early stages are quiet. Humble. Hidden. But eventually, what starts small must rise to carry fruit. And fruit comes with responsibility. That's the shift we're stepping into now, not just becoming something, but carrying something.

In the next chapter, we'll talk about that weight, about spiritual authority and what it means to live not just for yourself, but for the people God's entrusted to you. The seed you're nurturing today? It's not just for you. It's for others too.

Keep tending it. Keep trusting Him.

---

[17] Clear, J. (2018). Atomic habits: An easy & proven way to build good habits & break bad ones. Avery.

God is still growing something in you, even if no one else sees it yet.

The Growth Cycle of Purpose

LIVING IT OUT: CULTIVATING WHAT'S BEEN PLANTED

Faithfulness in hidden seasons lays the foundation for fruitfulness in the right ones. Here's how to stay rooted in the soil God has placed you in.

► **What Has God Planted In Your Life Right Now?**

Slow down and ask:

- What assignment or dream has God entrusted to me—even if it still feels small or buried?
- How am I being invited to honor it daily with faith and patience?

► **Who's Walking With You In This Season?**

- Don't walk through the soil alone.
- Reach out to a brother and ask: "What seed has God planted in you right now?"
- Pray for each other's growth—even if nothing is sprouting yet.

► **What Truth Are You Rooting Yourself In?**

Carry one of these scriptures into your week:

- **Galatians 6:9** "Let us not become weary in doing good, for at the proper time we will reap a harvest if we do not give up."
- **Zechariah 4:10** "Who dares despise the day of small things, since the seven eyes of the Lord that range throughout the earth will rejoice when they see the chosen capstone in the hand of Zerubbabel?"

- **Mark 4:31–32** "It is like a mustard seed, which is the smallest of all seeds on earth. Yet when planted, it grows and becomes the largest of all garden plants, with such big branches that the birds can perch in its shade."

The seed you steward today could become someone else's shelter tomorrow.

....

The seed you steward today could become someone else's shelter tomorrow.

....

chapter nine

Living a Legacy

Legacy isn't just what you leave behind—it's what you build right now in the lives of those around you. It's formed in quiet sacrifices, everyday choices, and the values you plant that continue to grow even after you're gone. The word "legacy" often feels reserved for the wealthy, the powerful, or the famous. But in the Kingdom of God, legacy starts with faithfulness. Not status. Not accolades. But obedience.

What kind of story are you writing with your life? Not the story others read online—but the one your children, your friends, your community will carry forward?

If your life ended today, what would echo in the lives of those who knew you?

If your life ended today, what would echo in the lives of those who knew you?

MORE THAN INHERITANCE

In our world, legacy is often tied to inheritance—money passed down, businesses handed over, or names engraved in stone. But biblical legacy is something far deeper: it's about generational impact and spiritual inheritance. While an earthly inheritance might pass down property, finances, or family heirlooms, a spiritual inheritance passes down faith, conviction, and a living example of what it means to walk with God.

It's the treasure of knowing Him and the truth of His Word, assets that can't be lost to economic collapse, stolen by others, or diminished over time. In Scripture, spiritual inheritance is about leaving those who come after you with a clear path toward God's promises, a well-worn trail they can follow when life tests them. It's about walking so closely with God that your footsteps become a path others can follow.

King David, despite his flaws, was called "a man after God's own heart." His legacy wasn't perfection—it was pursuit. David stumbled, sometimes in ways that had devastating consequences, yet his pattern was always to return to God with a whole heart. The Psalms reveal his relentless longing: "As the deer pants for streams of water, so my soul pants for You, my God" (Psalm 42:1). He chased God's presence in triumph and in failure, in the throne room and in the wilderness. That unwavering pursuit, not a spotless record, was what marked his life and shaped his legacy. He left behind not just a throne, but a trail. Solomon built the temple from David's blueprints, a project I can imagine David dreaming of but never got to see completed. Even though God told

David he wouldn't be the one to build it, David poured his energy into preparing every detail: the plans, the resources, the organization of the priests and musicians. It's a powerful picture of legacy, investing in something you may never personally step into, trusting that the next generation will carry it forward. Generations later, Jesus, the Son of David, would embody the covenant God promised him. That covenant, found in 2 Samuel 7, was God's declaration that David's throne and kingdom would be established forever. This wasn't just about an earthly dynasty; it was a prophetic promise pointing to the Messiah. Jesus came as the model of that promise, the eternal King whose reign would never end.

David's faithfulness, even in his imperfections, became part of God's redemptive storyline for all humanity. That's the kind of legacy that lives beyond your lifetime. His hunger for God shaped a nation and left a spiritual imprint that carried forward to his descendants.

Even when David's descendants failed, turning to idols, making destructive choices, God remained faithful to His covenant with David. Legacy isn't built on controlling outcomes or ensuring that every generation walks perfectly. It's about planting seeds in faith, entrusting them to God's care, and resting in the truth that His promises endure beyond our weaknesses.

What kind of father do you want your kids to remember? What do you want your presence to have planted in others?

LIVING WITH THE END IN MIND

One night as I was tucking my son into bed, he looked up at me and asked, "Daddy, can you pray that God helps me become a good man?" That moment stopped me in my tracks. It reminded me that legacy isn't just formed in public decisions or long-term plans; it's passed down in whispered prayers and quiet moments of trust.

That night with my son, when he asked me to pray that God would help him become a good man, I realized he was already absorbing what matters most, not from my speeches, but from my posture toward God. Those moments teach more than any sermon. They tell our children, "You can bring your hopes, fears, and future to God, and He listens." It's formed when our kids catch glimpses of what matters most to us, even when we think they aren't watching.

When we live like tomorrow isn't guaranteed, our values become clearer, our investments become more eternal, and our presence becomes more intentional. I think of my sons—how the words I speak, the tone I carry, and the habits I model are forming something in them every day. I don't just want to leave them money or memories—I want to leave them a spiritual foundation: a way of life marked by courage, integrity, and communion with God.

LEGACY IN THE ORDINARY

Legacy is built when no one is watching. It's forged in your responses, your prayers, your patience. It's the seed you plant in the soil of your kids' hearts when you show up one more time, even when you're tired.

Your legacy is not built on someday. It's shaped by every small yes to faithfulness today.

Jesus lived just thirty-three years. His public ministry lasted only three, but His legacy is eternal—because He lived with full obedience in every moment. In those three years, He poured His life into twelve men: fishermen, tax collectors, and others with no worldly influence. He invited them into His daily rhythms, shared meals with them, modelled prayer, challenged their thinking, and walked with them both in their failures and their victories. By the time He returned to the Father, these twelve had been transformed into leaders who would carry the gospel to the ends of the earth. This is the power of intentional, focused discipleship: investing deeply in a few so they can impact many for generations.

LEGACY IS INVESTING IN PEOPLE

We live in a culture obsessed with instant results and short-term wins. The kind of legacy that truly lasts rarely makes today's news, but it shapes the headlines of the next generation, because the people we invest in will be the ones making those headlines. Their decisions, courage, and character will ripple outward into homes, communities, and nations.

According to Barna research, only one in three Christian men feel equipped to lead their family spiritually.[18] This means many are navigating fatherhood, leadership, and faith

---

[18] Barna research, only one in three Christian men feel equipped to lead their family spiritually -- Barna Group. (2020). Five essentials to engage today's men. Ventura, CA: Barna Group.

formation without a map. That's why the call to build something that lasts isn't optional; it is essential. As pastor Jon Tyson puts it, "The most important thing you'll ever do in your life may not be something you do—but someone you raise."[19] Your legacy is not a brand or a platform—it's a life multiplied through others. Jesus modelled this perfectly. Though He ministered to thousands, Jesus devoted His deepest energy to twelve men. And through that investment, ordinary men became courageous, Spirit-filled leaders who would change the world. That kind of transformation is only possible when we see people, not platforms, as our greatest legacy.

I've known men whose names never made headlines—but whose lives planted faith, strength, and peace in everyone they touched. Men who didn't leave behind platforms or large estates but left behind people whose faith was stronger, whose courage was bolder, and whose lives were anchored in hope because of the time invested in them. Simon Sinek once said, "A star wants to see himself rise to the top. A leader wants to see those around him rise to the top."[20] That shift—from proving yourself to pouring yourself out is the essence of legacy.

This is the kind of man I want to be—one who invests in a legacy that lasts. Legacy is often invisible while you're

---

[19] Tyson, J. (2021). The intentional father: A practical guide to raise sons of courage and character. Baker Books.
[20] Simon Sinek once said, "A star wants to see himself rise to the top. A leader wants to see those around him rise to the top."

living it—and undeniable once you're gone. We plant the seeds, but God is the one who makes them grow.

BECOMING A MAN WORTH FOLLOWING

Legacy isn't about trying to impress the masses—it's about leaving fingerprints of heaven on the lives entrusted to you: your kids, your spouse, your coworkers, your community.

You don't have to be perfect, and while presence matters, it's not just about being in the room; it's about bringing life when you are. True presence listens with humility, leads without control, and creates space for others to grow. A man can sit at the table yet be miles away in spirit if his heart is closed or his influence stifles. Legacy is forged when your presence consistently breathes encouragement, wisdom, and godly direction into those entrusted to you.

So, ask yourself:

- What am I planting?
- Whom am I shaping?
- What will echo when I'm gone?

Your life is saying something—make sure it's a message worth repeating. "The righteous lead blameless lives; blessed are their children after them" (Proverbs 20:7).

**Legacy leaves heaven's fingerprints on
the lives entrusted to you.**

Let your legacy be love. Let it be integrity. Let it be the echo of a man who walked with God—and left a trail worth following. Even our past failures can become part of our legacy, when we let God redeem them into wisdom, humility, and compassion for the next generation.

The mistakes we regret can become the very testimonies that give hope to someone else. A moment where you once fell can be the lesson that helps another man stand. Your scars can become signposts, pointing others away from the same pitfalls.

And here's the good news—it's never too late to begin shaping that kind of legacy. Legacy isn't reserved for the man who has done everything right from the start; it's forged in the man who chooses, today, to walk in step with God. You can start now. You can plant new seeds now.

As you turn the page into the next chapter, remember: your legacy will not be sustained by sheer willpower or relentless striving. It will be anchored in something far deeper—grace.

The Long Walk: A Legacy of Faithfulness

LIVING IT OUT: YOUR LEGACY STARTS NOW

Legacy is shaped by the daily seeds you plant, not by titles or recognition. Here's how to live it with intention.

▶ **What Are You Planting?**
Take five quiet minutes and ask:
- What patterns or habits are shaping my influence right now?
- Are they helping those around me grow or holding them back?

▶ **Who Is Learning From You?**
Identify one person in your life who's watching you closely.
- How can you model encouragement, guidance, and godly direction for them this week?
- Where can you let go of control so they can flourish?

▶ **What Truth Anchors Your Legacy?**
Choose one scripture to carry with you this week:
- **Proverbs 20:7** "The righteous lead blameless lives; blessed are their children after them."
- **Galatians 6:9** "Let us not become weary in doing good, for at the proper time we will reap a harvest if we do not give up."
- C.T. Studd: "Only one life, 'twill soon be past; only what's done for Christ will last."[21]

---

[21] Studd, C. T. (n.d.). Only one life, 'twill soon be past. In Poems of C. T. Studd.

chapter ten

Anchored In Grace: Living the Long Game

There's a quiet pressure that follows many men—not the kind that screams, but the kind that subtly whispers: "You're behind. You should be further by now."

It's the voice that doesn't celebrate steady progress—it critiques every unfinished task. It measures your worth by output. It makes rest feel like laziness. And over time, it wears down even the strongest men. I know what it's like to carry that pressure: to set ambitious goals, chase vision, and wake up wondering if you've made any progress at all. I know what it's like to look at where you are and silently think, "I should be more consistent. I should be better by now."

But that's where grace steps in—not as an excuse, but as an anchor. The life God has called you to isn't sustained by hustle—it's sustained by Him.

So, What Is Grace?

Grace is not just God's willingness to overlook your mistakes; it's His active presence and power enabling you to live in freedom and purpose. It's the undeserved favor of God, yes, but also the ongoing strength to walk with Him day by day. Grace meets you at your worst, but it doesn't leave you there. It pulls you out of self-reliance and into communion with Jesus.

For many men, the idea of grace has been clouded by religion, rules to keep, boxes to check, a scorecard to maintain. But grace invites you into relationship over regulation. It's not a spiritual loophole to excuse apathy; it's the steady current that carries you forward when your own strength runs dry.

Paul writes, "My grace is sufficient for you, for My power is made perfect in weakness'" (2 Corinthians 12:9). That means grace is more than a pardon; it's a power source. It's the fuel for endurance, the guardrail that keeps you from drifting into pride or despair. And when you understand it, grace frees you from the crushing weight of self-made success, rooting you instead in God's faithfulness.

In *A Long Obedience in the Same Direction*, Eugene Peterson says, "It is not the intensity but the constancy of faith that matters."[22] Grace is what makes constancy possible. Left to ourselves, we either burn out trying to keep up the intensity or drift when the emotional high wears off. Grace steadies our steps when passion fades. It empowers us to keep showing up—not from sheer willpower, but from the overflow of God's strength working within us. When you are anchored in grace, faithfulness stops being a sprint fueled by adrenaline and becomes a steady walk paced by His Spirit.

---

[22] Peterson, E. H. (2000). A long obedience in the same direction: Discipleship in an instant society. InterVarsity Press.

I've had seasons where faithfulness looked like getting up early to pray—even when I was exhausted. Other times, it meant resting instead of overcommitting. Grace kept me grounded—not in performance, but in purpose. It reminded me that my worth was not tied to my schedule, my output, or the applause of others. In seasons when I pushed toward overcommitment, grace whispered, "You are not the savior; rest is part of obedience." In seasons when I wanted to disengage, grace stirred me to take the next faithful step.

For me, rest meant more than a day off, it meant trusting that God could work while I stopped. It meant leaving space for Him to speak, to replenish what hustle had drained. Grace taught me to measure my days not by how much I did, but by whether I walked with Him through them. The men who finish well don't always run the fastest—but they run with rhythm. They pace themselves by God's grace. They return, again and again, to the One who strengthens their hands for the long haul.

ROOTED FOR THE LONG HAUL

There's a reason Scripture uses agricultural metaphors so often: trees, roots, pruning, harvest. It's because spiritual formation isn't microwave quick; it's planted deep in the soil and proven over time. And grace is the soil where those roots grow. Psalm 1 says the man who delights in the Lord is "like a tree planted by streams of water, which yields its fruit in season." Grace plants you where living water never runs dry. It guards you from the burnout that comes when you try to bear fruit out of season. Without grace, you'll either force growth before its time or wither under the weight of constant striving.

For the man grinding in obscurity, grace says, "Your season will come, don't uproot yourself chasing faster results." Trees don't hustle—they draw deeply from their source. And in the long haul, it's grace, not frantic effort, that produces lasting fruit.

. . . .

Without grace, you force growth early or wither from striving.

. . . .

"Grace is not opposed to effort; it is opposed to earning. Effort is action; earning is attitude."[23] When Dallas Willard wrote these words, he was distinguishing between working hard from a place of security in God's love, versus striving to earn His approval. Effort is part of discipleship: we still show up, still act, still take steps forward, but the motive is love, not fear. Earning says, "If I do more, God will accept me." Grace says, "I am already accepted, so I can give my best without fear of losing His love." That difference changes everything; one path leads to exhaustion, the other to freedom.

LIVING FROM GRACE, NOT GUILT

The danger for many men isn't that we don't care; it's that we care too much and carry the weight alone. I remember a

---

[23] Willard, D. (2006). The great omission: Reclaiming Jesus's essential teachings on discipleship. HarperOne.

season in my own life when guilt became my fuel. I'd missed a few mornings of prayer, and instead of returning to God with honesty, I doubled down on performance, serving more, committing to more, pushing harder, hoping to make up for what I'd "failed" at. But guilt is a terrible motivator. It can push you to act for a while, but it can't change your heart. Eventually, the weight becomes too heavy, and you burn out.

**The danger for men is caring deeply
without sharing the weight.**

Grace, on the other hand, doesn't just pat you on the back and say, "try again." It goes deeper; it transforms the way you see yourself and God. When I say grace "absorbs your shortcomings," I mean it takes the very places you've fallen short and covers them with Christ's finished work. It doesn't ignore them; it redeems them. Grace trains you to choose again by freeing you from the fear of failure. You can take the next step, not because you've mastered everything, but because you know you're already secure in Him.

STEADY OVER SPECTACULAR

We live in a world that glorifies big wins and viral moments, but legacy isn't built in highlight reels. It's built in the daily decision to keep going when no one's watching. Grace is what keeps you steady when the applause fades. It's what allows you to keep loving when the people you thought would run with you have slowed down or walked away entirely. Sometimes grace toward others means releasing them without bitterness. It means blessing them as they go, even if their leaving stings.

Other times, grace means accepting help when you'd rather handle everything alone, or having the humility to admit you can't do it all. Grace doesn't lower the standard; it strengthens your stride. It keeps you walking with God in the mundane seasons and through the lonely stretches, confident that His presence is enough.

I once heard someone say that failure doesn't have to be the end if one finds the courage to get back up again. That's what spiritual longevity looks like, not perfection, but perseverance. Not burnout or bravado, but a quiet strength that chooses faithfulness over flash.

LIVING IT OUT: ANCHORED IN GRACE

Grace is not just a finish-line gift; it's the steady rhythm that carries you through every season. Here's how to keep walking the long game without burning out or running ahead of God's timing.

▶ **Where Are You Running From?**
Take five quiet minutes and ask: "Where am I moving from pressure instead of grace?"
- What areas of my life feel fueled by guilt or performance?
- Where is God inviting me to slow down and trust His pace?

▶ **Who Reminds You Of Grace?**
Reach out to one man you trust and ask:
- "Where have you seen God's grace hold you steady in a hard season?"
- Share your own struggles and listen without rushing to fix. Walk together.

▶ **What Truth Are You Anchored In?**
Choose one of these scriptures and carry it with you this week:
- **2 Corinthians 12:9** "My grace is sufficient for you, for my power is made perfect in weakness."
- **Hebrews 4:16** "Let us then approach God's throne of grace with confidence, so that we may receive mercy and find grace to help us in our time of need."

- **Matthew 11:28–29** "Come to me, all you who are weary and burdened, and I will give you rest […] you will find rest for your souls."

Final Charge:
Faithful to the End

THE COMPASS STILL POINTS TRUE

You began this book standing in the wilderness, compass in hand, unsure if the needle could be trusted. Maybe it spun wildly, leaving you restless. Maybe it lay buried in your pocket, ignored for too long. Or maybe you never realized you were carrying one at all. That's where we started—acknowledging the quiet ache for direction, the longing to know your life is aimed at something that truly matters.

Now, here at the end, the compass hasn't changed. It still points true. What has changed is you. You've walked through wounds, confronted lies, unearthed purpose, and wrestled with grace. You've seen that the path forward isn't about perfection—it's about presence: presence with God when His silence feels long, presence with your family when distractions pull at every side, presence with your brothers when it would be easier to isolate. And that kind of presence costs something. It costs comfort. It costs ego. It costs time you thought belonged to you. But that's the cost of becoming whole, the cost of walking in step with the One who calls you. It's not about never stumbling, but about learning how to rise, how to keep showing up, how to walk faithfully when the way isn't clear.

This journey was never about reaching a finish line. It was about awakening to who you are, to the God who calls you, and to the truth that your life carries weight beyond what you can see. The compass you hold is steady. It will still point north tomorrow. The question is, will you keep trusting it when the path gets costly?

—⊛—

In the fire of adversity, God has been shaping you, not to destroy you but to strengthen you—like metal returned again and again to the flame until it can bear the weight it was made for.

Some of the most impactful lives in history came from men who found their compass not in ease, but in adversity. Nelson Mandela spent twenty-seven years in prison. He lost freedom, status, time, and opportunity. Yet it was in that confinement that his purpose was clarified. He emerged not bitter, but resolute, not broken, but strengthened. Mandela once said, "I have walked that long road to freedom. I have tried not to falter... I have taken a moment here to rest, to steal a view of the glorious vista that surrounds me. But I can only rest for a moment, for with freedom comes responsibilities..."[24]

His years behind bars didn't diminish his influence; they distilled it. They purified his resolve. He was a man who didn't lose sight of his purpose even when everything

---

[24] Mandela, N. (1994). *Long walk to freedom: The autobiography of Nelson Mandela.* Boston, MA: Little, Brown and Company.

external was stripped away. Mandela didn't find his purpose in prison—he held onto it throughout prison.

Viktor Frankl, a Holocaust survivor and author of *Man's Search for Meaning*, spent years in Nazi concentration camps. He watched fellow prisoners die of hopelessness long before their bodies gave out. But Frankl discovered a principle that reshaped how he understood purpose, one that continues to challenge how we see it today. He wrote, "Those who have a 'why' to live, can bear almost any 'how.'"[25]

---

[25] Frankl, V. E. (2006). *Man's search for meaning* (I. Lasch, Trans.). Boston, MA: Beacon Press. (Original work published 1946).

Acknowledgments

One of the most humbling parts of writing a book is realizing how many people helped carry it from a faint idea to these printed pages. This wasn't a solo climb; it was built through the prayers, encouragement, and faith of so many people who believed before I could see it clearly myself.

To my editor, Jennifer Hill, thank you for seeing through the early chaos of scattered ideas and half-finished stories, and patiently chiseling them into something coherent and alive. Your clarity, wisdom, and care for words helped shape this book into what it was meant to be.

To Team Bailey: my incredible wife, Gabrielle, and our two energetic boys, Kalino and Kawika. You are my heartbeat. There were countless nights you asked, "Dad, is your book done yet?" and your excitement kept me going. I'll never forget the day Kawika saw an old thrift-store book titled The Awakening of Man and shouted, "Dad! Is this your book?"—not yet, son, but soon enough.

To Dr. Ralph E. Plumb, thank you for always lifting my vision when weariness tried to settle in. Your steady encouragement and reminders to "keep the bigger picture in sight" helped me stay the course. To Jim Orred, thank you for your spiritual guidance and the countless times you've challenged me to walk deeply with God rather than rush ahead of Him.

To David Gava, for every call, prayer, and word of motivation during the hardest stretches, you have no idea how often your timing was divine.

To my brother Jacob, who prayed for me through quiet seasons when progress seemed invisible, thank you for being the definition of faithful brotherhood.

To Evan Bartel for your unwavering support, and to Maarten, who travelled from Papua New Guinea to Australia and then all the way to Canada just to help film a short video for this project, your commitment still humbles me.

To Evan, Dean, and the guys in Winnipeg, who showed up for the very first men's gathering before this message had a name, thanks for helping me see that this vision mattered. And to my global brothers and friends, from every season of life, who cheered me on from afar, thanks for believing in the message before it was ever bound between covers.

I'd like to say a big Thank You to Michael and the Illumify Media team for bringing this book to its final print.

Finally, to God, the Author of every chapter, the One who never stopped writing when I wanted to give up. This book belongs to You. Every story, every breakthrough, every quiet moment of grace—it all began and ends with Your faithfulness.

You've endured silence, those seasons when heaven felt muted and prayers echoed back unanswered. Yet even there, roots went deeper. Faith was built not in noise, but in stillness, where trust grows without applause.

You're discovering the gift of brotherhood. Men who sharpen you, who hold your arms high when they would otherwise fall, who remind you that manhood is not a solo climb but a shared ascent. Brotherhood doesn't erase battles—it makes sure you don't fight them alone.

And yet, even with brothers beside you, your path is still your own. God doesn't form copies, He forms sons. Your story may move slower, quieter, or through valleys others never walk, but that doesn't make it less holy. Comparison tempts you to despise the process, but God is not rushed. His timing is about formation: growing roots before fruit.

That's why purpose often starts like a seed—small, hidden, breaking open long before it bears fruit. In the soil of waiting, God roots you deeply enough to sustain what He intends to grow. And when you see legacy through this lens, it shifts everything. Legacy isn't built on comparison or quick wins. It's built in the slow obedience of today, the prayers your children overhear, the seeds of faith you plant when no one is watching, the courage to keep trusting when timelines disappoint.

But legacy takes more than passion. Passion burns hot but fades quick. What will keep you steady isn't adrenaline or applause—it's grace. Grace is not God overlooking your failures; it's His presence and power enabling you to stand, to breathe, to begin again. Grace steadies your stride when passion fades. It whispers that you are held, even when your strength is gone. But grace doesn't remove the cost; it redeems it. It teaches you that presence is not passive; it's the daily choice to stay engaged with God, with others, and with the moment, when it would be easier to retreat. The one who remains faithful when no one's applauding. Presence isn't just about staying--it's about standing firm. And when you choose to stand with grace and conviction, you become the kind of man others can follow.

⸺ ❧ ⸺

Brother, this is your charge: keep showing up. Keep trusting the compass in your hand. Keep walking when the path feels unclear, when the weight feels heavy, when the silence lingers longer than you hoped. Keep leaning into brotherhood. Keep planting seeds of legacy you may never see fully bloom.

You are not behind. You are not forgotten. You are being built. And the quiet, faithful life—the one anchored in grace and marked by presence—is still the most powerful story a man can live.

That's the picture I want you to carry as we close. Legacy doesn't come through applause, titles, or endless striving—it comes through faithfulness. Through the long obedience in the same direction. Through grace that steadies you when strength runs dry.

So, as you step forward, don't drift back into survival mode. Don't bury the compass you've reclaimed. Don't settle for half-alive when God has called you to a life marked by courage, purpose, and faith.

The world doesn't need more men who can perform under pressure. It needs men who can stay faithful under fire. Men who rise when it would be easier to hide. Men who choose grace over grind, brotherhood over isolation, presence over performance.

You are that man, not because you're flawless, but because God is faithful. His Spirit in you is more than enough to steady your hands and strengthen your stride.

So, step forward. Keep showing up. Build the legacy no one else can build. Your children, your brothers, your community—they don't need you to be perfect; they need you to be present in a way that brings peace, strength and stability—not controlling, but consistent, not flawless, but faithful. Your story is already echoing beyond you. Live it well.

The world needs men who stay faithful when pressure becomes fire.

KEEP CLIMBING

You did not finish this book by accident. If something stirred in you, that matters. Awakening The Hero Within is not a finish line. It is a turning point. The climb continues from here.

START HERE

Everything connected to this journey lives in one place. Access the companion workbook, legacy tools, guided experiences, events, and discounted bulk purchase options for churches, leadership teams, and organizations.

CONTINUE THE CLIMB

Join weekly conversations and teaching through video and podcast.

Find Teko on social media - @iamtekobailey

Listen To The Climb Podcast

LIVE FULLY. LEAD BOLDLY. LEAVE A LEGACY THAT MATTERS. — TEKO

About the Author

Teko Bailey is a husband, father, and faith-driven coach who helps men rediscover their God-given identity, rise to their calling, and live with purpose. Shaped by his roots in Kingston, Jamaica, he has served in ministry and community development across Sierra Leone, The Caribbean, Hawaii, and beyond. Today, he lives in Canada, with his wife Gabrielle and their two sons, Kalino and Kawika.

Whether mentoring leaders, coaching men through hidden battles, or walking alongside fathers in their journey, Teko carries a vision to see men lead with courage, walk in wholeness, and build a legacy of faith. When he's not speaking or writing, you'll find him biking with his family, listening to Bossa Nova, Reggae, or sharing good conversation over ethnic food or coffee with people from all walks of life.

Connect with Teko:

Website: **Tekobailey.com**
Social Media: **@iamtekobailey**
Podcast: **The Climb (with Teko Bailey)**